RUNNING FROM BEARS

A NEW YORKER'S WILD AWAKENING IN ALASKA

ADRIANA JAYMES

Praise for RUNNING FROM BEARS

"Wow! This story struck me on so many levels. Even the most successful of us women have a history of neglect or abuse that made us seek validation outside of ourselves in career or partners. Without healing our internal wounds, the lives we created as an escape aren't sustainable, and this story was a perfect storm for just that. Realizing our own self-worth sometimes happens in the harshest of realities, but it's FOR us. Every woman should read this!"

—DANIELLE DON DIEGO, MD,
Author of *Self-Care RX*

"An honest story of uncertainty, trauma, regrowth, and independence, Jaymes lays bare her fall from grace in 2008 and what led her to do a 180 in her personal and professional life. A must-read for anyone who has been in an abusive relationship, Jaymes' openness and resolve will be an inspiration to all those that read her incredible experience."

—KATHRYN BURMEISTER, ESQ,
Author of *Overcoming Addiction to the Status Quo*

"Intimate, vulnerable, and courageous, Adriana Jaymes' riveting memoir is a gift that reminds us all that the love we seek lies in abundance within."

—TARA FORD, PA-C,
Preventive Medicine Specialist,
Author of *I Am Not the Only One*

"When it comes to true psychopaths, getting out of such a relationship requires quite a skillset. Ultimately, we must learn to disable then ignore them. Bravo, Adriana Jaymes."

—CAPRICE HAVERTY, PH.D.,
Forensic/Clinical Psychologist

For my grandmother, Ida, who said,
"Just go, Adriana, just go!"

CONTENTS

ACKNOWLEDGEMENTS

I've always looked for adventure: Both in love and in life. All of them taught me, but one of them changed me.

In 2012, I met my Alaska man. In 2014, I moved to the great state for what I believed was the love of my life. He was, but it turned out he was not the love. I was, and I finally found the person I had been searching for all my life: Me!

Alaska is simply the most beautiful place I've ever seen. The mind cannot process the vast, natural complexity and ever-changing light, flora and fauna I saw while living in the boreal rainforest of the Tongass in Sitka, Alaska. I made friends, learned to fish and walked in forests never seen. I kayaked in clear jellyfish and salmon laden waters, within fifty feet of grizzly bears. Rafts of otters and spraying whales surrounded me on boat trips and walks near the water. The place spoke to my soul at the deepest of places. I'm forever changed.

In the end, my Alaska man is a small part of my story.

I have to thank my grandmother, Ida, for telling me to "Just go." She had always imagined travel to exotic destinations and read daily about so many of them. Sadly, her life did not take her to the places she so dreamt of. She gave me the courage to board planes and "just go." She developed my love of books and reading from childhood. My gratitude for having been her offspring is unending and I'll never stop pining for her.

Thanks to each and every Sitka friend and stranger who supported me, stood by me and shared their own truths about personal relationships and past experiences with the person I'd come to their town to marry. It took courage to speak the truth and it made a world of difference to me and my recovery. Also, thanks to Kris Hoffman, my dear friend and trusted advisor during the hardest of days and the aftermath. Keith Perkins showed me the truth about laughter and friendship, at a chance meeting after the devastating landslide of 2015. Wendy Lawrence and Bryan Bertacchi wrapped around me, took me in and made me family. The days of boating and a Christmas High Seas Adventure in a sixteen-foot skiff will not be easily forgotten!

I'd also like to thank Jocelyn for his support and belief in me.

Finally, Candi Cross! I'm not sure how she moved into my universe just when I needed her, but she did. One of the most skilled story interpreters to walk the earth lives and breathes life into the stories she hears. I hope this is just the first of many projects we'll take on together.

INTRODUCTION

Poking the Bear

*"The bravest are surely those who have the clearest
vision of what is before them, glory and danger alike,
and yet notwithstanding, go out to meet it."*
—Thucydides

ALASKA IS BEAR country, with approximately 30,000 of those fur-ry-faced, dangerous creatures roaming the state. Before my first run-ins, I must confess, I kind of thought of them all as cute, cuddly teddy bears. Bears and eagles in Alaska are as common as pigeons and rats in New York, however, with bear mauling happening fre-quently—and that's not cute.

Teddy bears and grizzlies are very different creatures. A teddy is the most comforting mother substitute to millions of children. Usu-ally, a teddy is worn and at times, missing essential parts. Eyes fall out, buttons get lost, fur is rubbed off from years of a child holding tightly onto that thing that offers comfort and solace, security and warmth. Cuddling with that little bear is so often a cherished child-hood memory that some adults still have their original and worn bear many years later, after a mother who kept it safe, returns it to its rightful owner.

Other bears, the kind that live on the island of Sitka, Alaska are not so constant and predictable. The largest of the bears, the brown or grizzly, thrives in Sitka. They roam the island at will, pillaging garbage cans, breaking car windows, and scratching at people's doors and trying to gain entry through kitchen windows. Backyards, driveways and public parks may be taken over by these kings of the island.

Most people sense danger soon enough and divert their activities to avoid them at any cost. Sometimes though, a bear will just be there and take a person by complete surprise. *Whoa* to the man who meets a sow with cubs in tow. This is one circumstance where attack is most common.

When a bear does attack, it is fearless and often scalps the person, going straight at the head and face. Isn't that what an abuser does to his victim? He finds the place his victim is most vulnerable and emotionally "scalps" her, in an effort to disable any defense mechanism she might have. An attack to the face or to the victim's clothes or other belongings is rather personal and threatening.

Some bears are tentative, running when confronted after tearing into garbage cans. An air horn might be all that is needed to send one on its way. Others are barely bothered by the rubber bullets shot by police and have to be destroyed. A gun is a safer choice. A big gun is even better!

Still, a brown bear on the "small" side is 800 pounds and can tear a human to shreds in moments.

Each year in Alaska, humans are attacked by them, usually surviving, but with severe wounds and psychological damage from the trauma of the powerful attacks. People are most often simply caught unaware and when a bear charges, it covers ground quickly. Data says thirteen yards in a second is not uncommon.

One cannot outrun a bear. If one tries, the bear will see them as prey and charge them with a full-on attack. Since bears are visible daily, hikers and outdoor folks in Sitka try to be prepared with bear spray, dogs and air horns. Most don't believe in guns, but they are safer companions than a pepper spray that only serves to piss off the beast more. For the record, I was a rootin' tootin' gun-carrying woman when I resided in Sitka. They even have a pistol clinic especially tailored to women, so I was in good company. "Bears" were a common topic in our chick chat.

The difficult thing is the unpredictability. A bear might sniff and move on, or attack. In these ways, bears remind me of men, and one in particular that my story portrays. Brian, what a once-delicious, devilish, and very dangerous man to all women in his horizon.

If you ever feel like running away, suddenly leaving—no note, no warning, no shit to pack—go to Alaska, a fascinating and special place, totally unique and strange in its isolation, with beauty unparalleled by most other places. But be on the lookout for bears… and Brian.

CHAPTER 1

My Boom and Collapse

"Making money is a hobby that will complement
any other hobbies you have, beautifully."
—Scott Alexander

HOW MANY WOMEN just take off and run? Most people would never risk it. Too many things hold us down. Houses, cars, kids, and two hundred pairs of shoes. It all can't be thrown in the trunk! In my case, circumstances changed drastically when the perfect storm of events took place at once, demanding I look at my life and check its direction.

I lived in the Hudson Valley, which extends 150 miles above the tip of Manhattan. Designated as a National Heritage Area, the valley is steeped in history, natural beauty, culture, and a burgeoning food and farmer's market scene. Among many attributes, it's the oldest wine-producing area in the country, and the magnificent scenery inspired artists whose works became the Hudson River School of Painters. It's not a little-known nest of natural beauty. *Lonely Planet* describes the Hudson River Valley as "a real city break, with leafy drives, wineries and plenty of farm-to-table foodie options."

National Geographic Traveler named the Hudson Valley one of the "top 20 must-see destinations in the world".

Despite its charm and prestige, I never loved the Hudson Valley due to the stains of past relationships and family issues. Then I got pregnant with my son. It was more important to have my son be close to family, with lots of children around, so I didn't leave. I gave up the young years of my life that I thought would be dedicated to adventuring with a backpack and wanderlust to give my son stability, so he could grow up to be a productive human being with a lot of love in his life. He grew up and went to college.

It always amazed me that an investment of fifty dollars and forty hours of classroom education could plop me into a career with unlimited income. The real estate industry is filled with swindlers for this very reason, but in my almost thirty years in the business, I found that most agents acted with integrity and honesty despite their built-in conflict to make the deal or starve.

Being an attractive and bright woman with good people skills always landed me in great places. I have had the best of things and experiences, but I took them for granted, squandered my money, and thought I would always have the things I wanted. I started out as a hard worker and became someone who worked a little less hard for a whole lot of money, which spoiled and distorted my reality. The crash was a true reversal of fortune and in some ways, I felt I had it coming. I never internalized being gifted or even talented, yet with a high school diploma, and a lot of hard work, I had managed to earn over $200,000 per year.

At first, my success was unfamiliar, but as the years passed, my income growing each year, I became used to the money and was casual and careless with my spending. Money is a privilege I would come to learn, and once accrued, must be handled with respect if one means to keep any of it. Mostly I just spent, buying, traveling, and providing a high-quality education for my only child. Saving much never entered my mind. To be totally transparent, at least I wasn't alone in that state of mind. In 2020, during the coronavirus pandemic, the Federal Reserve reported that 39% of Americans didn't have enough money on hand to cover a $400 emergency, and they reported this same figure years ago.

I bought and sold homes as if they were as disposable as plastic water bottles, making profits and spending those, too. I still get off on the high life. Elite hotels, clothes, food and restaurants enjoyed with loved ones is a fine existence. Sharing one's good fortune is satisfying. Broadway shows, Macy's, Talbots, and Nordstrom ate up my checks, along with manicures and pedicures complete with champagne at Beauty Bar, waxing, hair appointments, furniture and art. In essence, you can have a lot of unrestrained fun with $200,000. I became the life my income supported. It never occurred to me that anything could change that I wouldn't have the power to control. This way of life was also getting exhausting. Stuffing myself with material things, I felt empty and unfulfilled. My life-pipes were clogged with meaningless items and mindless entertainment.

I can recall cashing $30,000 commission checks and spending them in less than one month. Hell, once I cashed a $65,000 check. It disappeared in one blur of manic splurging and a Bahamas vacation.

To this day, I wonder if others have shared my experience of living this way. Was my carelessness a subconscious disregard for myself, my talent and my hard work? After all, as hard as I worked to earn it, I worked even harder to keep spending it. I felt some guilt, as if I did not deserve to have that much money. Once or twice, a small voice in my head asked, "What if this ends someday?" I pushed that thought away as quickly as it had appeared. I should have listened.

Staying busy dominated my routines. I did not want to think about my life in any depth, but looking back, there were so many choices I had, so many things I could have done to ensure a better future. A bit of education, some research and maybe professional advice could not have hurt. I made stupid choices and did not invest my hard-earned money and use it as a tool to make more.

My husband, a rugged, handsome man of the John Wayne variety, and I, had been together for four years. He owned a farm, and he was a solid person in the community. The moment things shifted financially with the crash in 2008, he vanished. In a way, the mortgage meltdown was a gift because I could have stayed with him for many years, not knowing his true motives for being with me. Lessons learned come hard, and I lost everything in the meltdown. It was my third divorce and I was the common denominator.

My career of twenty-five years imploded. Real estate had come to a grinding halt and my second job in the mortgage business fizzled after over twenty years, too. My income plummeted to under $50,000. It was a desperate time.

My bottom was when my son, with no money, found himself locked out of his college dorm, and determined to stay there, slept in the courtyard in Manhattan, in the middle of frigid January. I was powerless to help.

I was in shock and completely unprepared to face the unhinged and rapidly collapsing real estate market, and the loss of the handsome income I had earned since my early twenties. John Wayne left me alone in a huge house in the Hudson Valley, on six acres with a riding mower and lots of fancy china. Soon, I could not pay for it and it went into foreclosure. Six million people lost their homes. My story is just one of those.

Fortunately, the foreclosure process is protracted in the state of New York. It took five years and that gave me time to think. I was mostly frozen and scared though, living each day not knowing when a man with a gargantuan padlock would come and drag me out of my home.

Never the defeatist, I started volunteering for a literacy organization and doing local talk radio to help others facing foreclosure. The calls poured in.

People had desperate stories of losing a job, only to obtain another at half the pay and then losing that one, too. Pregnant women sobbed as they faced the loss of their homes and unemployed husbands. I talked to hundreds of people staring down foreclosure. One guy cut his finger off out of rage from being out of work for a while. He was a rugged guy who wasn't a very good communicator. Because I was educated in finance, I knew how to talk to the banks to get them to help these people. I saved his house. Then I saved my sister's house.

Finally, my broker in the same office bellowed, "You can't go on this radio show anymore. Our office can't handle the phone calls!"

I had saved at least fifteen homes. There was no work for me. I was going through a divorce. Every loan I had as a mortgage broker in the pipeline had been rejected. I used my own desperation to help other people save their homes. I went back to college and earned my bachelor's degree. But none of this put food on my table or helped my own crisis.

With the cash flow clogged, I had no idea who I was. Then several people in my life died, including my dad and my rock, my grandmother. Relationships were going nowhere. Dating was leaving me emptier than ever and my bachelor's degree, at a cost of $62,000, had zero impact on getting a job. I really didn't want one anyway, so I found ways to derail the few opportunities that did come my way. I knew I did not belong anymore. The problem was, I did not know where I did belong. Confusion and despair were not unfamiliar companions in those days.

After hundreds of hours scanning job ads online and having mailed just as many resumes, I realized none of it fit; there was not one job posted online that I wanted. That's why nobody called!

I had no answers. I was lonely and craving something new, something real. Everything that had ever happened in my life added up to this moment and came skidding onto the pavement with no brakes.

CHAPTER 2

Romantic Perfection

"A kiss is a lovely trick designed by nature to stop speech when words become superfluous."
—Ingrid Bergman

WHEN I WAS a child, I was smitten by John "Grizzly" Adams. A big, strong, fun-loving man overseeing the wilderness with a harmless (cute) bear companion and helping passerby in the forest—what's not to love? To accompany my fixation, I have always taken to rugged men who know how to get practical things done. To be clear, my attorney in New York City frantically called me to come and change his toilet seat! I've met plenty of suited up metrosexual men who pay people to change lightbulbs and tires. I didn't feel safe with them, needless to say.

In 2012, I went online randomly Googling Alaska. The state seemed to call me. Then I discovered *Alaska Men*, a popular magazine created by a woman named Susie Carter, who highlights single men in Alaska, or "husband material". Most are attractive and represent a sample of the available men in the state. Bearded bears are pictured either holding a fish, fishing, or on a boat, with or without a gun. These are Alaska men! Odds for a woman are good, it is said about Alaska men, but the goods are odd. Single men in Alaska out-number single women significantly at a ratio of 108 for every 100 women. Surely, I could find my own husband material.

The men looked friendly and down to earth, unlike the worka-holic and egocentric male persona so prevalent on the East Coast, per my experience. I wrote to three of the Alaskan men—two became friends and one would rock my world so hard that I would eventu-ally trade in my Valentino studded heels for Xtratuf's brown rubber boots. Brian lived in the remote fishing town of Sitka, 800 miles north of Seattle and accessible only by plane or boat. His emails to me professed his undying love and dedication; his desire for a good life with a woman who would love him. It sounded like my dream. For six weeks, we corresponded nonstop, before I couldn't stand the wait any longer and jumped on a plane to Hawaii with a trip to Sitka, before my scheduled return to New York.

A few weeks before my departure to Hawaii, he wrote me this email that seemed sincere and made a glowing impression on me; especially the part about him being a gentleman:

Good afternoon,

It's lunch time and my workload is down to a dull roar so I thought I would write you a bit. My phone is new; it's the new iPhone, so I think it is perhaps my location when we have spoken that might have been the problem. I was lying in bed with my eyes closed when we spoke so that I could concentrate on our conversation and feel close to you.

Kauai is very casual. Getting dressed up for me is putting on linen pants and a linen shirt, and that does not happen often. My shoes generally come off the day I get there, and it's flip flops the whole time. It will be an interesting packing dilemma for you. Packing both for the Tropics and Alaska. If you want to put your northern clothes in a box and ship them here, that might work.

I have no problem with you coming to Sitka. I just worry that it may be way different than what you are used to. My home is in the middle of a four-year renovation. Some of the windows do not have sills, and one bathroom and the kitchen are still circa 1960, right down to the bake light panels. It is very comfortable, just not yet to where I see it in my mind's eye. I guess this has more to do with me wanting to make a good impression on you than anything else. It's a good thing you are dating me and not my home!

Yes, it is a little weird compressing six months of dating into a couple of weeks. I am much different on vacation than when task orientated.

I am grateful that you are willing to step out and take a chance. I can imagine what your friends are saying. I can assure you that you will find me respectful, attentive, and a gentleman. It is how I live my life. I find myself looking at your pictures daily. Your spoken words rattle around in my head on a regular basis. I count myself lucky to have somehow crossed paths with you.

I look forward to showing you what little I know about Kauai. It is an enchanting place. Lovely, lush and fairly rural for Hawaii. Perhaps you will become as

enchanted with it as I have become.

Adriana, I just want to say thank you for being you. I look so much forward to meeting you and holding your hand and experiencing your smile in person.

XO Brian

I was in love with Brian before we ever met, but when he sauntered up to me in my hotel courtyard, I was stunned by his beautiful, bright blue eyes, white teeth, and warm hug as he placed a fragrant Hawaiian lei around my neck. He was taller than me at 5'8", a big man over 6", and I loved his smile. He was a sight, and I was impressed, maybe even bowled over. To be honest, my whole body was on fire. Could this be the ONE?

Often, as a child, as I laid on the grass on a blanket, listening to the sound of bees buzzing around, clover and dandelions at eye level and ants crawling up, tickling my knees, I could hear the faint roar of airplanes high above the summer sky. I made a favorite fort in a closed area of trees, sweeping the "floor" and building shelves where my daffodil-laced mud pies, stolen from neighbor's gardens could "cook" in my imagined double oven. I loved to play "house" and I still do.

Much of my fantasizing about a knight in shining armor was done here in my fort, and for my entire life, I have been a romanticist and believer in that one true love. Call me naïve, but despite evidence to the contrary, I could not give it up. Fueling that fantasy, the next two weeks were as close to perfection as one could get. I did not notice that Brian did not do much to impress me or even appear to want to. For my part, I did not mind. This was a man I enjoyed simply being close to, to look at. He was a beautiful sight. I just enjoyed him as he was, which, in and of itself, fascinated me. Throughout my love life in New York, my needs seemed never-ending, so I was as mystified by this newfound simplicity as anything. Sitting side by side, each with a book, was as close to heaven as I could have imagined.

We enjoyed each other's company as we drove carefree around the island and half strolled, half hiked Hanalei Beach, a vivid blue-green unlike any color I had ever seen. I had no way to know I could have been any woman in the form of breathing, warm, curvy flesh there with Brian. I filled a blank space. Today, I know that to him, it mattered not who I was; being a female and there for his needs and desires was enough.

Hawaii is so impressive that little external stimulation is necessary. Its energy is palpable, vibrating, jungle-like. Movies like "South

Pacific" and "Jurassic Park" filmed on Kauai have drawn scores to its lush, green landscape. Wild chickens roam Kauai's roads and visit the local restaurants like paying guests. Rainbows appear intermittently throughout the day alternating with warm, soft rain showers.

Some of the most beautiful days of my life happened with this man. One breathtaking scene was a rainbow and giant golden sunset falling into the sea behind a stranger posed on a cliff as if he were there solely for that moment. We walked miles of deserted beaches and fell in love. We spent three weeks together.

It was a long first date and unconventional, but we both loved every second of it like a drug of love.

Six weeks later, Brian flew to see me in New York.

And then I chased my husband material in Alaska six weeks after that.

CHAPTER 3

Sharing Regular Diets of Disappointment

"I'm drawn to bad romances."
—*Lady Gaga*

THROUGHOUT OUR CORRESPONDENCE in between breathless escapades in person during those early months, I learned a great deal about Brian's upbringing. He was born in the 1950s by parents, Dolores and Walter, an optometrist. They had met in Chicago years earlier. Brian was the youngest of three children, with two sisters; they lived on a boat, the Researcher, first in Juneau and then Sitka, where Brian was born, until the family could own a home of their own.

One story, relayed to me by Dolores (or "De"), is that one of the children fell overboard into the frigid waters, making life aboard the last straw for her. She insisted they get a home and by all accounts, they did soon after.

Dolores and Walter had a strained marriage and by 1963, after a "scorched earth divorce" according to Brian, both remarried, with much happier outcomes.

The children did not fare quite as well. In the middle of the night, Dolores awakened the children and told them they were going to Disneyland; to get in the car. She and her husband, Bernie, kidnapped the children and moved to Nebraska. According to Brian, it took two years for their father to locate them. Once located, they disappeared again until Walter could finally find them and take legal action to win them back. Dolores told the kids their father did not love them, and she did not permit any communication between them while they were out of Alaska.

The children, missing their father, went to court and testified as to their mother's cruel and intolerant treatment. Walter was awarded custody and took the children back to Alaska to live with him and his second wife. Dolores never forgave the children for this "betrayal" of her. Nor could she understand why they had "made up all the lies about her".

For a while, things seemed happier. Walter was a sort of Renaissance man. He was a doctor, an artist, and drove about town in his classic Jag and wore an ascot from time to time. He ran for senate and lost. To this day, his widow, married at least four times, still carries his last name and calls him "the love of her life". Many of his paintings are still hanging in various buildings around town and the family is also in possession of quite a few. He had an interesting eye, and painted his subjects, whether humans or landscapes, with clarity and straightforwardness.

Medicine, art, family were not enough to appease Walter or stave off critical depression. He committed suicide in 1973 after returning from a family trip of a year in Europe, for reasons known only to him, the details of which are blurry. He simply sat in his car in the garage, closed the door, started it up and died from carbon monoxide poisoning. He didn't leave a note. He took his life just a few weeks prior to his only son's fifteenth birthday.

Brian spoke lovingly about his father and cast his mother in harsh light, often telling stories of her mental instability and cruel verbal treatment, calling him a "shitty kid" repeatedly, yet after crawling into his "loving" father's lap, relayed a story about having been beaten with rebar and hiding in the woods for an entire day after he committed a minor infraction.

If we see our past clearly, we might not be able to view our parents with as much love as we'd like to. Sometimes, it's easier to stick with our own version, flawed as it may be.

It was a tough life in Alaska during the 1950s. Milk had to be powdered and eggs were often spoiled by the time they reached Sitka. Fresh produce in this area was limited, and to this day, excessively expensive. Lacking modern materials, house projects that required them were rigged and people made do the best they could. It was still a pioneer life in many ways. Brian inherently knew that wanting certain things did not guarantee ever having them. Sometimes, he decided, it was just better not to want them at all.

I felt a great deal of compassion for the little boy in Brian and wanted to care for him and heal his wounds of maternal and parental abandonment by loving it away. I wanted to somehow show him the universe is not unforgiving but a wide-open space, a cornucopia filled with all of the things we want and are readily available.

My own mother, an unwed child when she gave birth to me, never seemed to understand my almost desperate need for her love. I recall feeling resented, even before birth, and was aware on some level that she had not wanted me. My mother had started pumping babies out, with no real thought of what it would require to take care of us. She was sixteen years old; my father, twenty-one. From the earliest age, my job in life was to take care of people. Take care of the other kids. Set the table. Polish my father's work boots and iron his shirts. Feed the dog. My mother was never neat and tidy, which doubled my chores.

Therapists have told me that my mother was insanely jealous of me. My mother was short and stout, and I was tall, thin, attractive. When we were out together, people would stop in their tracks and beam repeatedly, "Karen, your daughter is beautiful!" Despite their enthusiasm, she would roll her eyes toward the sky and respond, "If I hear this one more time," sighing. They looked at me with sadness or horror that my mother would respond like this both when I was a child and as her adult daughter.

I made a lot of money in my thirties and forties. My son, Trevor, went to private school. We drove showy cars, had a beautiful home. I represented a kind of package that she could not touch because of her own choices. In turn, she would call me "ugly" feigning humor, hoping it would penetrate. And it did. Who doesn't want a doting mother? On top of that, she became a religious extremist.

Think of the most insanity you can think of in a religious person—one of the Jehovah's Witness variety. That's my mother. She led by domination. I had a rebellious personality, so I would fight her in second grade and get the shit beat out of me. I didn't want to go to Kingdom Hall meetings, and she would literally lay on me—all of her body weight holding my little body down—so she could dress me. The more she did this, the more I tried to fight her. My behavior shamed her sense of safety and high standards of morality on strict *Bible* teachings. Having participated in premarital sex, a serious sin in the eyes of Jehovah's Witnesses, she was already a cheapened version of the faith. I knew that it was an all-encompassing, cultish religion abusive to women. I refused to get baptized, and my mother had an "unclean" family as a result of that. Never mind all the other shit that went on in our house!

This was the setup for the rest of my life; spawned from a bitter, narrow mother and an alcoholic father with no sense of responsibility. Mother turned to this religion and became a freak. She craved control. The Scripture gave her this. She had been Catholic before and asked the church for answers about my disabled brother's debilitating condition and why we were on this earth. The Jehovah's Witness doctrine pointed to Scriptures that made her feel safe.

Mom was not mean like Dolores was, but still, I had my damage. All of us, intentionally or not, damage our offspring. My father was emotionally, physically and verbally abusive. At ages sixteen and twenty-one respectively, my parents were not quite adults themselves. Without more than a high school education, and parents with less, they were flying by instinct and example. My own father, an illegitimate child and the product of an extramarital affair with an unwed mother, had been placed in what was then called a foundling home, until at age two, his maternal grandparents arrived from Scotland to collect him and took him back with them to raise him until he was a teenager. Then they brought him back to New York, where they bought property in Rosendale, a small village. Dad reunited with his mother, this glamorous woman who always wore elegant clothes and paraded around with different men. She had never married.

A child abandoned physically or emotionally at such an early age often sustains permanent damage that is life-lasting and hardly ever heals. Our family typically sat down to dinner daily when I was small. My mother felt it important that we see our dad, uninterrupted at least once each day. Often, the conversation would be about us begging dad to take us to Dairy Queen for dessert, especially in summer. He was fun that way and indulged us more than most fathers probably would. Sometimes though, if we had a poor report card, or had been disobedient, there would be hell to pay.

I had come home one day with the letter "N" on my report card. I believe it meant "needs improvement". Math, a subject I struggle with to this day (thus, no savings!), was becoming more challenging each year and I was falling further and further behind. I was not a lazy child; it just made no sense to my brain. It was like reading a foreign language with no training.

"Young lady," my father said, "I see you had a bad report card." Teacher comments also said I needed to work harder and talk less in class. My mouth in many ways has been a two-edged sword, propelling me to success as an adult in a sales career, but as a child, the amount I talked, and my tone were frequent causes of punishment and grounding.

The knot in my stomach was growing with anticipation over my father's attention and threats. "You are going to get a beating after dinner," he said. I swallowed hard, sick to my stomach and not able to eat a bite as I envisioned my punishment.

I remember little more than having my pants pulled down, alone in my bedroom with him and going over his knee for a few whacks with the belt. The shame of being naked in that position was far worse than the beating. It has stayed with me to this day. Parents teach children in a million little ways about shame and accepting treatment far more severe than is appropriate.

My father was so effective at frightening me that when he and my mother fought, I would gather the other children in my bed and hold them in a circle, and nobody was allowed to make a peep, for fear of him coming for us next.

One time, after he fought with my mother and slammed my younger, handicapped brother into a wall like a rag doll, I called my grandmother and she and my grandfather drove an hour to come and check on us.

He was verbally abusive and once yanked me out of the bed while sick with flu because my mother was also sick and unable to do the dishes. He made me stand there, dizzy and with a high fever, washing the dishes while he insulted me about the size of my behind. To this day, I have a fear of possessing a larger-than-ideal rear end. "Your ass is just like your mother's," he said. My mom was a curvy woman, but his remark left me with a lifelong phobia, as if after having had five children, one's body would not have been affected. Most men love their wives' curves.

Such was the dynamic in my childhood home. Some days, it was the flavor of ice cream, a devil dog or a ring ding for dessert. Other days, it was extreme discipline and verbal abuse. I just never knew. Remember, they were kids themselves and of a different generation. Still, it was frightening not to know.

Each day, as I arrived home from school, the first thing I would look for was my dad's van in the driveway. If it was there, I had intense stomach cramps and diarrhea. If not, I knew I was safe from his verbal and perhaps physical abuse for a few hours. If he was not home, I felt free and light, ready to enjoy my after-school hours at will.

Abuse is one thing, neglect is another. To be fair, my parents were so young. I was their first child. I am sure they did their best, but at times, when I was very sick and should have been taken to a doctor, I was not. I became accustomed to the feeling of not "mattering" and of feeling disregarded. It continued through many of my adult relationships as I learned to take care of myself and to function alone in that capacity. During my pre-teen and teen years, the neighborhood girls often excluded me from their clique. It hurt so badly and felt vaguely familiar to be rejected. As I became a woman, other women did not frequently warm to me and I know now, it was because I was so fragile on the inside. I had to project zero vulnerability on the outside to protect myself against emotional harm I believed would come if I showed who I really was.

Once, a therapist remarked that it would have been easier to just get socked in the face every day. At least one can brace for it.

I soon developed a cough and digestive problems due to the uncertainty of my circumstances and learned to hide when I could, immersing myself in reading or fantasy, lying still and quiet in my bed in an effort to remain unseen. Dinner time remained a stressful event as my father seemed to take pleasure in making me jump up from the table for things he might want or demand. I barely took a bite when he needed a knife, salt, pepper, a fresh napkin or some odd item from the kitchen counter.

This practice ended one evening when my grandmother, my protector, was visiting us and noticed his behavior. In her customary kind but insistent way, she instructed him to leave me alone and let me eat my supper. My father always held my grandmother in high regard, spoke respectfully and never resisted or spoke up to her that I can recall. In retrospect, his wife's mother was more of a mother than his own.

I am sure all of the parents, Brian's and mine, did what they knew best. To be fair, physical punishment was more accepted then. Both sets of parents used it. As children and adults, psychological abuse is even more damaging and much less visible. Some of us don't have the capacity to rebound as others might, and so the damage is deeper and more permanent. With our respective histories, I believed I understood Brian's pain and believed we would both heal our wounds by directing all of the unmet love and affection we both so desired to each other, much like the way I loved my own child.

After losing Walter, Brian told me that his stepmom withdrew from the children. While understandable due to her grief and being left to raise five children, it probably took every ounce of her resources to cope. The children, however, were left to fend for themselves. Brian turned to drugs and alcohol and took his anger out on weaker, smaller kids, beating them up in the schoolyard and enjoying every moment of his power over those weaker, according to a former high school mate who knew him back then. This is how a bully comes into being.

Brian worked and saved his money, ski bumming for a few years between high school and college, keeping mostly to himself and intentionally without attachments. He grew up and moved on, damaged and estranged for years from his biological mother, who showed little love or affection, and his stepmom's withdrawal and the loss of his dad, the man who he saw as his savior and hero.

Trauma beginning early in life and continuing through the teenage years reduces a person's chances for healthy, successful relationships. While challenged in my own ways by the environment in my home as a child, at least I had a loving grandmother to spend my summers with, someone who lavished me with the love and attention a little person needs in order to be whole and feel loved.

Both of my grandmothers were exceptionally good to me. My paternal grandmother was always dressed to the nines and frequently showed off her antique finds in the sleek apartment she lived in alone. I used to go to her apartment for New Year's Eve celebrations with my maternal grandparents.

Brian was not so lucky. Being fed a regular diet of disappointment, one begins to lose touch with physical sensations that become unbearable because humans are unable to cope with this sort of pain for long periods of time. They may take actions like engaging in promiscuous sexual behaviors, drinking, taking drugs, or starvation to numb or turn off those feelings by shutting down their own physical sensations and as a result, lose touch with their physical presence. People often experience a reduced capacity to function in their bodies and organs may not work as well as they might without the trauma and disassociation from one's physical body. If lucky enough to find treatment later in life, optimal functioning may be restored. In my case, homeopathic treatment helped me cure a case of chronic shingles and chronic infections that had plagued me for over twenty years.

CHAPTER 4

Threatening the Wildlife

"It has been my observation that parents kill more dreams than anybody."

—*Spike Lee*

WE CELEBRATED CHRISTMAS, alone, together in Brian's house that first year. I had purchased several gifts and even brought him a valuable painting a close friend and well-known Hudson Valley artist had done. In turn, Brian gave me a calendar. Yes, I know—a glossy paper calendar to hang on the wall in exchange for fine art to hang on the wall. Perhaps this was some small gesture from a higher power to remind me that I didn't need to be showered with gold and silver if I had true love?

Brian introduced me to both his mother and stepmother. His stepmom was warm and kind, whispering sweet things to me about Brian and his father in her kitchen. "He's had his problems," she said, "but he is a good man." "Walter was the love of my life," she told me, and she talked about her second husband openly and often, even in the presence of her present husband, who did not show even a hint of reaction to her incessant praise of the man who had chosen to abandon her by suicide. Their lovely A-frame home was warm, and it felt cozy and familiar.

It had been the home she lived in with Walter and the kids many years ago.

She made me feel so much a part of the family. I belonged. Dolores, his biological mother, in contrast, was acerbic and cool. Brian took anti-anxiety meds prior to us going to her home for Christmas dinner. She made no effort to make me feel at home, and her demeanor was more formal and stiffer than Brian's stepmother. We did manage a laugh or two and I left feeling like the visit had been a positive experience…so far as I had been told it could be.

It was a relief after about three hours to leave her contemporary, smoke-filled home with a killer ocean view and tobacco-stained ceilings, with blinds she kept mostly closed to the stunning Alaskan scenery below. "You were perfect," Brian said, releasing a heavy breath as we left. I took it as compliment that he felt I measured up to his mother's standards, although I had no idea what they were.

Nothing else in my life was fulfilling. The multitude of dating options in the New York area seemed mundane and boring. I wanted out from under, to be away from all of the expectations and demands I felt from others. I had nowhere to go. Brian, through his attentive emails, phone calls and visits, made me feel loved and wanted. I was lost and on the rebound, desperately wanting to find the love that would sustain me for the rest of my life.

Still, I was looking for things outside of me to make me whole. Lessons still waiting to be learned loomed in the distance. I believed in love in the truest sense of the word, and it was becoming more urgent that I find it. More than any other thing, I wanted love and would go to any length for that goal. It was the first time in my life I would throw all my chips in. I had not learned that what I was searching for was not something outside of myself, so any effort to find it could not ultimately be successful. It is true that until we find our own wholeness, it cannot be found in another.

I was spoiled and overindulged for a long time by the attention men lavished on me. I was rarely without a suitor and often had to offer a firm "No!" when strangers approached me in an effort to secure a date.

Powerful and older men with money were drawn to me. I had always earned six figures in a real estate career that rewarded charisma and good communication skills, yet I was tired of the self-serving attitudes of the men I kept meeting, who were on power trips or driven by their careers. Several had left their wives for me. The men I knew always had some private agenda that included me, just not in the way that had meaning in my life, forcing relationships faster than I wanted to move, without much concern for my feelings to develop. I tried to adjust but always hit the same spot in the road where I was lonely, exhausted and mentally detached from trying to fit myself into somebody else's life plan. It was mostly my fault, not theirs. I am sure each one gave me what he thought was his best. It just never fit, so I had to go on without them.

Looking back, I can see the distance between New York and Alaska allowed my love for Brian to grow in the absence of daily interaction and conflict. The daily challenges of life, moods and individual preferences that can, at times, stress a relationship, did not exist. I could make the fantasy what I believed it was. It was so easy. I interpreted Brian's lack of pushiness to be consideration, when in fact, he was not a risk taker and did not have much personal investment in our relationship. He was wooing several women and kept as many balls in the air as he could.

This might be a good time to read the book, *The Sociopath Next Door*, by Martha Stout, PhD, as a companion reference.

CHAPTER 5

It Takes a Fur Sale

"The truth does not change according
to our ability to stomach it."
—*Flannery O'Connor*

ADULT RUNAWAYS ARE misunderstood. I'd bet my friends are split down the middle when they talk about it.

"Did she have a breakdown?"

"She must have burned out."

"She really lost it!"

I had to GO. It was a visceral feeling of agitation. Staying still was not possible. Everything I knew was gone, and the hours became clear that change was necessary to grow. I felt pigeonholed and stuck in the box of expectations of everyone who knew me. Change was the only way out.

There was something in me that had always required permission or at minimum, others' opinions. I hesitated and wavered in my own desires because of self-doubt and fear. Prior to this time—the crash, another divorce, Adriana's rock bottom—it was not humanly possible for me to do anything different. I don't know why, but it was not.

My house was being taken by the bank. It was late 2013. When they finally did come, locking me out of the main part of my home, in one swift act of defiance, my son unscrewed the magnificent bronze and Moroccan stained-glass chandelier from the dining room ceiling to mark the end of this long chapter.

I gave away most of my things, one by one, thinking of the recipients as keepers of my life in moments. Selling personal items one by one becomes emotionally overwhelming. When I could take no more bargaining from Craigslist callers, cash laid in my hand at the recognition of a good deal, I listed my $6,000 fur coat for $25 on Craigslist. I'm not even sure I blinked twice before the buyer raced up my driveway, grabbed the coat from its rack, stuffed the cash in my hand and peeled out, tires screeching, accelerator to the floor as if he were off to the Indy 500!

I still chuckle at that sale today. It somehow makes disposing of thousands of dollars of possessions bearable, to merely laugh. And I did. I let out a deep-belly laugh like never before. I think I was laughing at my own life. Total release. Haven't you heard that laughter, orgasms, sun, and dancing stave off depression?

I condensed a 4,000 square foot house into a 10 X 10 storage unit and headed to Florida in my car with very little money, two suitcases, no job and the credit card of a man who was much kinder and more generous to me than I ever deserved.

There was some numbness involved. Brian, listlessly stirring in Alaska, had no idea of what it was to undertake such a process and expected me in Alaska post haste. I was in love with a man in Alaska but was loved by a man in New York. It was time to decide. Men have always been my problem. They won't leave me long enough to get anything done!

Florida was my first stop. I stuck my toe in the water and headed to the home of my childhood friend. We began our healing together. Her second husband had recently died; preceded by her first husband, to cancer. She persuaded me that it was too soon to make the decision to go to Alaska, that I needed time. She offered me her home without hesitation and told me to stay as long as I liked. She meant it. We could have grown old together.

Thank God for friends. Those months with Helen probably saved my life. She opened her home to me and asked for nothing in return. I had never felt suicidal, but then I was so devastated, crushed by the circumstances of life, I surely did not recognize how deep my grief ran.

For the next six months, Helen and I laughed, yelled, drank wine and beer, ate candy and ice cream, and healed. Bags of Reese's Peanut Butter Cups disappeared in one fell swoop. She got pneumonia, I made chicken soup. I got shingles. A professional therapist, she gave me massages. Through it all, we laughed and cried, napping frequently as we both got stronger despite days where one or both of us never got off the couch.

More women should do this sort of thing.

We hated men together and I even ran one off the property when he came looking for his wife, after a fight, with a dozen roses. The house was a sanctuary for angry women. We shredded them on Helen's front lawn, whipping them bare on the spiky crabgrass for the neighbors to see. It might have looked a bit trashy as the newly washed slipcovers for the couch were drying in the sun, draped over the lawn furniture after Helen laughed so hard the night before, she really did wet her pants and spit her beer out of her mouth and nose, soaking the covers completely.

"You're offensive" became my operative phrase with Helen. She was raucous and wild, seeming like a feral cat to me at times.

My sense of propriety was her target, and she rarely failed to disappoint, provoking me as she took pleasure in her hilarity, knowing exactly how to elicit the desired response. It was a once-in-a-lifetime experience and for six months, we were teenagers again, not the menopausal women we were on our way to becoming. It was irresponsible and totally appropriate that we kissed our younger years sweetly goodbye as we moved into the next phase of life.

During this time, I had decided not to pursue the Alaska relationship and backed away from Brian, stopping communication completely.

When he did not hear from me for several weeks, he messaged me on Valentine's Day saying he loved me. I cried and knew I loved him, too. Fate knocked on the door of my heart in this moment. Simultaneously, I did not know that he was with a former lover he had flown in from Anchorage for the holiday and was with her as he wrote me a message:

I, too, believe strongly in commitment. And absolutely through thick and thin better and worse.

To be fair, I had a dinner date that day, too! Looking back, neither of us was totally committed. I was trying to move on and had been doing some dating in Florida and New York, which turned up a few crazy religious nuts, one with a personality disorder and a couple of seemingly normal but badly damaged guys, both emotionally and physically. Can someone please design a fucking dating app with a mental health checklist in which you also have to attach a clean bill of health from a medical doc and a shrink? I'll invest.

During the Valentine's Day communication, Brian and I decided he would come from Alaska to Florida for us to decide what to do about our lives going forward. I had not seen him for a year and wanted him to come to Florida before I made the decision to move to Alaska and marry him. We made plans for a week in Key West for his birthday in April.

He wrote:

Adriana, you need to know that I am speaking from the heart when I say I am looking for a woman that I can fully commit to. After being single for about five years and being in the dating scene a little, I have a strong desire to meet that special someone

*and give everything I have. I long for a relationship into which I
can give and share my whole self.*

Women know. We know sooner and more often than men. I saw
a few troubling signs but decided that he just needed to be "trained".
Trained for commitment, for perfection, for the title of THE ONE.
Yeah, right! This is a critical error in judgment. None of us should
have to drag a man behind us when they don't know or choose not to
make good decisions that are respectful or are inconsiderate of others
who are participating.

On Brian's birthday, we headed to the beach and after a short
while, decided it was not the way to spend our day. I guess I figured
we would go back to the condo to shower and change before we
headed out. He suddenly announced he wanted to go to Key West.
Although we had made a visit to Key West as part of our plan, he
wanted to go now, today.

I had just gotten my period, was feeling ill and had only a bikini
and a sun dress with me. I really did not want to go but because it
was his birthday, I wanted to accommodate him and agreed to make
the trip. Again, this is the behavior of a people pleaser, heads up!

There were many bar stops, the first being a rum bar and finally, a
stop at a raucous Irish bar where I had to drag him out as I saw things
might be heading in a bad direction when suddenly, I saw a wild
look appear in his eyes. Was this going to be my first bear attack?
We ended the day with a birthday dinner at a fine white tablecloth
restaurant. I felt out of place in my beachwear, but I took it in stride,
and we enjoyed the evening.

I drove home after Brian got drunk and slept all the way back.
It was a slow ride on a two-lane road, and it took two hours. I was
sleepy and crampy, too, but the birthday boy appeared to be drunk.
I tried to dismiss my frustration.

Okay, folks, nobody with any level of self-awareness or sense of
consideration allows their partner to make a two-hour drive on an

unfamiliar and pitch-black road over the water basically alone while he sleeps off a drunk. That was painfully obvious bad behavior that should have set off alarm bells. It did not.

The next day, we decided to hang at the pool. We were alone and had sex in the water in broad daylight. Our passion and excitement blinded me. There was no doubt I was in love with him. Brian proposed that night, oceanside, but he had no ring. I should have known then that he made the decision on the spur of the moment, that he possessed no real stake in our relationship because he had not even bothered to buy a ring or insist that we buy one for the occasion. To his credit, he did offer me his own ring, which he had for years and held very dear. I did not take it.

Within a few days of his departure, my feet got ice cold and I called off the engagement from Florida, giving several reasons why I could not marry him. The real reason I did not want to go forward had to do with his daughter, who, at age 26 years old, still lived at home like a college kid. Brian could not seem to understand my discomfort at having his adult child sleep in the bedroom next to ours while we settled in with each other and developed our own routines and lifestyle. I simply did not want to develop my new relationship in the presence of my partner's adult child.

Brian quipped, "I think if you make the relationship conditional on this demand, you will just keep demanding!"

"I want our privacy," I stated flatly.

He acquiesced, and Allison turned out to be cooperative and respectful. We had a congenial relationship until the very end, even if we did not have much common ground.

The ringless engagement resumed.

CHAPTER 6

Manhattan to the Last Frontier

*"Love can sometimes be magic. But magic
can sometimes...just be an illusion."*

—*Javan*

THE FLIGHT TO Seattle was the first part of the journey to my new
life in Alaska. I mentally said goodbye to everyone and everything
I loved in Manhattan. The city would survive without me. Would
I survive without it? I didn't know yet. I was ready to conquer wild
Alaska. I didn't know the degrees of wild Brian though.

Landing in Seattle, we headed to the hotel where we would stay
the weekend for a family graduation party. Filled with euphoria, I
longed to meet my new family.

The first thing to strike me at Sea-Tac Airport was the lack of
"Fuck you's", shouting, car horns and fistfights among limo and cab
drivers seen so often upon landing at JKF. People were nice in Seattle. The vibe is chill. The color is black.

There is no intensity. No feverish movement to get to baggage
claim. No shoving, shouting or rushing ahead of others. People move
slowly and with courtesy. No visible adrenaline. It felt like landing
on the moon or witnessing a silent movie.

Having always been a big fan of prolific true crime author, Ann Rule, it was great fun to see the places she wrote many of her books about. Also known as "America's killing fields", the Pacific Northwest has a proliferation of serial killers and since it is my secret desire to be a fulltime writer someday, I fantasized about my new life and the family that would welcome me warmly, as well as the stories I imagined existed here, never stopping to consider the story would be my own.

Brian proposed again in our hotel suite with his grandmother's ring, which I wore to his sister's home. Bigwig Sis worked for a prestigious foundation in Seattle and had a home with lots of glass overlooking Puget Sound. The Pacific Northwest is grand and spread out. I love West Seattle and the Alki, along with Pike Place Market, Ballard and the other parts of the city I could see on that weekend. It's a bustling city but strangely devoid of the noise of Manhattan.

Due to Brian's sister being an employee of a well-known charitable organization based in Seattle, we always had rental cars cheap and super luxury accommodations when we visited Seattle, for less than a hotel room at any decent inn. Warm affections notwithstanding, apparently there are some perks to having bigwig family members.

During this weekend, we were ensconced in a suite at the Alexis Hotel in downtown Seattle, with every luxury and sweet treat we could desire. The shop in the lobby sold perfume, with exotic and unfamiliar scents worn by oil sheiks and princesses that cost upwards of $800 per bottle. *Someday*, I thought, *I will be back for one of these.*

Nobody at sis's house was very excited to hear of the engagement. In fact, they barely acknowledged it. I was crushed by the lack of consideration his family showed me that weekend.

His daughter, Allison, did not speak a word and glared at me with hostility the whole weekend. Apparently, Brian had not asked for her blessing to get married and she was so pissed off, she drank and sulked all weekend. Although quite beautiful in the sort of Uma Thurman variety, she did not make a pretty drunk; slurring words out of her crooked mouth and drooling lips, sneering in her stupor.

Bigwig Sis shushed me when I mentioned the engagement quietly and extended my hand. She made it clear I was not to ask for any attention. Apparently, she was so panicked that I would steal the thunder from her daughter who was graduating from high school, she could not even bring herself to offer a congratulatory toast. I was so shocked at the ignorant behavior of such a successful woman, I could not react on any level. It had never occurred to me that anyone of her stature could be so small. Welcome to the family!

The engagement was not off to an auspicious start and my fiancée did not seem to notice anything was off center. He did his best, though, to make it pleasant. We shopped at Pike Place Market, viewing some of the most spectacular displays of tulips, peonies and spring varietals blooming in one place. Brian loved flowers (husband material, in my book!) and bought several bouquets to bring home and to Bigwig Sis. We bought cheeses, meats and wine not readily available in Sitka. These shopping sprees would become commonplace for us. We bought all sorts of merchandise each time we visited Seattle; Sitka offered no such luxuries.

On the plane trip north to Sitka, Brian's daughter did not speak or offer to share her sushi, which she ate greedily in the seat next to the window as I hungrily looked on. I was not sure what was going on; except that Brian's stepmother alluded to the fact that his daughter was enraged at her dad's lack of consideration in asking her permission to marry me. A college grad and fully employed 26-year-old living with Daddy.

So far, these people seemed crude, lacking simple social graces and the sophistication of New Yorkers. We get a bad rap, but I truly never saw such awful manners. My husband material and I got in a tussle at Sea-Tac after going through airport security and being separated briefly on the way home. He had a sour face for hours until it gave way to calm as the plane lifted off.

Yes, I was heading "home" to begin my adventure. Nothing could dampen my spirits, dammit! I was finally going to live my rugged Alaskan life—whatever that really meant. I just ignored each red flag as it appeared, making it disappear with my hopes for a bright future.

Although it did not seem like one just yet, Alaska would prove to be the pivotal change and "adventure" I needed to shake my life up enough to get my attention and wake me from the coma of always knowing what comes next, what to expect. Nothing in the coming year would be anything I ever expected. There would consistently be stunning contrast between Brian's behavior and words. I cited Rumi's poetry to him:

There is a candle in your heart, ready to be kindled.

There is a void in your soul, ready to be filled.

You feel it, don't you?

He said that Rumi was his favorite.

I think you are quite a woman and have a depth that is unusual. The Rumi poem hit me where I live. Sometimes I have wondered, "Is she out there?"

CHAPTER 7

Into the Fire and Ice

"The most courageous act is still to think for yourself. Aloud."
—*Coco Chanel*

WE DEPLANED IN Sitka, and Allison departed for home in her broken-down truck without saying two words to me. Cars are not counted for much here and few have foreign upscale models. Most own trucks and even the wealthiest of people drive dirty ones, duct tape being a quick fix for minor repairs. Multiple dogs of the large variety ride shotgun or in the truck bed, even in the pouring rain.

Stepping off the plane, with a total of my two bags into the cool and very clean air of Alaska was noticeably different from the eighty-to ninety-degree temps in Florida and New York in summer.

Sitka is located in the Southeast portion of Alaska, off the coast of British Columbia, in the Tongass National Forest. It is North America's only boreal rainforest. Rain falls 80"-90" per year, and most days in Sitka have at least some rain; many have all-day torrential rain mixed with short breaks of sun. Encompassing close to 17 million acres throughout Southeast Alaska, it is an awesome sight to behold as the largest national forest in the United States.

The beauty of Sitka is a sight beyond description. Snow caps the mountains year-round, and with the sea in the foreground, it is a powerful vision to behold. Whales breach, splashing in the distance. The long summer days of sunlight make for an otherworldly experience.

Although New York is rich in beauty and many tourists come to hike and view the scenery, I rarely took advantage of it. It was certainly accessible, but my life was always so busy and occupied with meaningless family discord and mindless entertainment. I had to keep the money machine grinding and I knew no way to stop it. It seemed impossible to change course. Now, I felt like I could. All my senses stirred up at these amazing sights.

"Home" was less than five minutes away and we arrived with my two suitcases in tow, ready to head "out the road". "Dang", another Alaska vernacular, immediately came to mind. I noticed that no closet space had been cleared for me. Although Brian offered to make some room in his closet, I chose the spare room, painted peach with shiny silver trim and curtains of the fake silk variety hanging from the windows and began to move clothes out so that I would have a place to unpack. I was wounded by the lack of preparation for my arrival. I felt hesitant, a bit awkward perhaps, but happy to begin my life, so I pushed it away and smiled. I committed to this relationship, this location, for perhaps the first time in my life. Who needed banners, balloons…a little clear space?

The house, an older split level, was cozy and dated. With its dark brown carpet and painted paneling, I figured a woman's touch would spruce it up. Both kitchen and bathroom were born out of the 1960s and tired. Renovation was in our near future, I decided, but did not know quite how to get there as the outsider.

Brian gave me permission to move things around as I chose, but I was careful not to make too many changes since he was territorial and particular, even if his taste left a certain impression of early trailer park. Feng Shui did not seem to be a concern. A pair of 1980s tall stereo speakers and all electronics lined one wall, with the furniture against the other. Two partially dead plants were placed on either side of the room and milk crates held his record albums. Old lace curtains, abandoned by the former owner, hung on the windows.

The old wood kitchen table, another relic left behind, became a place of silence at mealtime. Brian believed in saying less at the table. In Italian homes, this was the main place of conversation, fights and laughter. Brian preferred quiet non-expression. An old and very lumpy blue velvet sofa served as our everyday seating. I tried not to grimace when he laid down on the couch, feet in my lap, as the sharp springs bored into my behind.

The bookcases housed his little ivory nick knacks, and everything was clean. Carved ivory is pricey in Alaska and only the Native Alaskans are allowed to carve it for sale. Baleen, as seen in many Alaskan homes, adorned the painted paneled walls, along with a huge ugly walrus skull and tusk I could never quite warm up to.

Such is Alaskan décor. An extensive art collection comprised of boats and fishing scenes and his late father's artwork was most impressive.

I tried not to get hung up on interior decoration. At least he could cook! Prime husband material category.

The population of Sitka is somewhere around 9,000. Almost one third Native American and the rest white, very few black and many Filipino, provide for an interesting and diverse dynamic. Native art murals and totems are present and visible in areas of town and parks.

While settling in, I read Michener's *Alaska*. With an appetite for knowledge, I wanted to know everything. The book provided insight into the Russian history of Alaska's first capitol and how the population came to be as it is. Alaska Natives suffered a great deal at the hands of the Russians and missionaries who came to convert them to Christianity. Many lost their faith and their cultural identities. Today, the culture fights to keep traditions alive in its youth and families. Michener wrote a good portion of the book in Sitka and I was able to see the house he lived in while he wrote it. It is said he was an arrogant and unfriendly type, but he did Alaska justice in his writing.

That summer of 2014 was the wettest summer on record in Sitka since 1940. One day, it rained almost three inches in twenty-four hours. Brian grew dahlias and although huge from so much daylight, they took a beating that year and bloomed late. It's hard to grow things in the Southeast, as the ground is gravelly, and the rain is unending. Each of those initial days, I wondered often aloud, *why do people live here?*

Wet as it was, I refused to change my clothes to adjust to the weather and I often suffered for it. Brian had a silly grin, seeing me drenched, trying to preserve my freshly straightened locks in a "do" that would not frizz. It was impossible. Wet is wet, cool or hot and my hair told the story of my daily fight with the weather. At least I had lipstick!

Temps were moderate. It rarely got very hot or very cold. I can only describe my waiting for the sweltering days of summer as disappointing at first. The seasons blended. One day, the thermometer registered a stunning 77 degrees and Sitkans used to the cool summer were sweltering, sunburned and irritable! I must have heard "Dang!" a thousand times from a hearty bunch who wore shorts, tees and often flip-flops in December, swimming in not quite fifty-degree frigid ocean waters if the air temperature reached fifty-eight. Teams play softball in downpours and spring games are appropriately called "mud-ball tournaments". Runners strap their little ones into strollers, wrap them in raingear and go.

It would take months for me to adjust, but slowly, I did, and slowly, little by little, I came to love my new home.

Summer is a busy time in Sitka. The town bustles as airlines add extra flights daily for the independent travelers and charter fishermen. If anything marks the change of seasons, it is the events that surround them. Instead of increased temperatures, the arrival of herring and the spawn marks spring; tourists, summer.

Cruise ships bring well-heeled tourists into town daily, sporting their high-end rain gear and Orvis clothes injecting fresh, alive energy into this otherwise sleepy, little town filled with art galleries and residents going about their daily lives. The ferry stops in most towns throughout Southeast, bringing independent travelers who decide to see Alaska on their own.

Rain arrives in torrents to mark fall and winter. Snow has hardly appeared the past two years. It had to be trucked in by rail in order for the Iditarod Trail Sled Dog Race, Alaska's famous race, to take place in 2016.

The art center of the Southeast, and often referred to as the Paris of the Pacific, Sitka draws children to its summer arts camp and musicians from the world over. Planes and boats make up a large portion of traffic in Alaska, as it has few roads and most of the small islands throughout Southeast are not accessible any other way. Sitka has five miles of road north and six miles south. One might use a tank of gas each month.

Life is unhurried. Few rush to accomplish daily chores and errands. Most stop and chat for what appears to be visits without a time limit. Such is the beauty of small-town life. People go out of their way to be nice. We saw each other often multiple times of the day and week. People talk. Being nice is a good idea because it's hard to forget past bad behaviors. Most drivers are considerate. Horns must not work in Sitka because I never heard one. Everyone values the town for its walkability and people enjoy walking after being kept indoors so frequently by inclement weather. I couldn't help but notice an ongoing war between cyclists not obeying the rules of the road and drivers.

Some locals didn't obey any rules...so I was told.

CHAPTER 8

Bad Boy of Sitka

"I have the reputation of being easygoing.
But inside, I'm like nails. I will kill."

—*Calvin Klein*

LETTERS TO THE editor of Sitka's newspaper flew and often, the writers were known for their submissions and given nicknames.

Brian had a notorious nickname, "BNR" as relayed to me on a flight by the resident who coined the term. Mr. BNR, or "Born and Raised" always started each of his letters with "I was born and raised in Sitka."

I heard many stories from local business owners who were well-acquainted with my lover and disliked him immensely. The tales were negative and shocking, but I brushed the content off as empty and envious. His family had planted a lot of roots in Sitka and he was a damned sexy man. I know, this speaks nothing of the rot that can be inside a person. Apparently, Brian had lost his temper with prominent fishermen and businessmen alike. Gossip is a blood sport in small towns, and behavior is best kept appropriate. Forgive my running on, but you must absolutely know this tidbit before coming to visit or live in Sitka.

The airport is tiny, and, on each flight, out-of-town folks gather and talk about where they are headed. The airstrip looks like an aircraft carrier in the middle of the sea. At the return gate at Sea-Tac Airport, where most fly through to return to Alaska, on Alaska Airlines Flight 67, the people have a certain rugged, ungroomed look and appear to be anxious to return to life there, without the speed and crowds we are all so accustomed to.

Wild beards on men and loose casual clothes of the North Face and flannel assortment are the rule.

My bright lipstick and high-gloss black leather designer purse never failed to gain confused looks on Flight 67. If I exchanged a few words with a fellow passenger, the remark was usually along the lines of "You live up here?"

Conversations and gossip were lively with many old friends crossing paths in the course of travel. The flight north is 860 miles and is referred to as the "milk run". With stops in Ketchikan, Sitka and Juneau, the flight goes on to Anchorage, its final stop, another 800 miles north.

"Right on", a common phrase, was often the response as one reported their travels. I giggled, remembering that phrase being popular on the East Coast in the 1970s.

On the day I returned from my first visit back to New York, it was a rare, clear sky with temps in the fifty-degree range. Given the date was March 1, and still winter, I was grateful for the clear skies and spectacular beauty I came to know in Alaska.

The Hudson Valley is a beautiful place, no doubt. Compare it to Alaska and it seemed dreary, tired and lackluster despite the culture and availability of anything one might want at any moment; this from a confirmed city girl. As traffic rushed by me, it occurred to me, *I am not this life any longer.*

CHAPTER 9

True Blood

"Compassion alone stands apart from the continuous traffic between good and evil proceeding within us."
—*Eric Hoffer*

TWO DAYS OF residing in Sitka barely passed before my future mother in-law was hemorrhaging and we headed to the hospital to meet the ambulance in yet another downpour.

The doctor arrived and talks with us, advising against another blood transfusion saying, "She will only bleed out and you are pro-longing her life. Let's talk to her and see what she wants." Such began a two-and-a-half-month stage of active dying, with Dolores flipflopping between wishing she would die and fighting to stay alive without any shred of grace, dignity or concern for her family. Dolores, or "De", was, in short, one of the meanest people I've ever met. She did teach me a lot about Brian, however.

As she lay dying, I was rubbing her feet and helping her on and off the toilet. Brian was emailing old girlfriends from her bedside, I would soon discover, to bring them up-to-date on her condition, and making no mention he was newly engaged.

Since we had no idea if De would live or die and she was hemorrhaging, she insisted she wanted to see her daughter, Denise, one last time. It had been at least ten years. Kathleen, her eldest child, had predeceased her many years prior in an auto accident, leaving behind an infant who was put up for adoption. Brian said the family gave the baby up, rather than allow De to raise (and abuse) another child as she had her own. Brian told me she had been abusing her grandson when he was a baby.

The doctor suggested it might be good idea to make those arrangements now. We called Denise and she vigorously resisted the idea. "I know Mom will harass me," she said, her voice jagged with anxiety. "And I am not up for it. I have not been to Sitka in ten years, and I cannot take the time off from work."

Brian did his best to convince her and made airline and limousine arrangements for the following weekend. Amazingly, she agreed.

Denise tried to be cordial and even offered to bring a cribbage board into the hospital to play with her mother, who readily agreed. The next day, however, after losing one of the ivory game pieces, she was blasted and criticized. It seemed there would be no remedy for the past.

The weekend was rough, each of us taking turns handling Dolores shifts. Her own granddaughter refused to be in the rotation. Denise stashed at her mom's house with no car, had limited options. We watched and waited for the shoe to drop. Brian, a bit tense, berated her for smoking inside the already tobacco-stained and smoke-damaged house.

She tried to keep an open mind, hoping for that last healing word, but after seeing her mother and being blamed and harassed for her choices as far back as childhood, as predicted, all she wanted was a drink. She tried any tactic to get one, darting into the Westmark Sitka Hotel for a pre-lunch double shot of whiskey.

Soon after, Denise asked to go to the Pioneer Bar at 8:00 a.m., just after the door opened. When we stopped for gas, she leaped out of the car and broke into a quick trot to get into the convenience store, even buying me a little bottle of gin as a gift. If my mother had ever reached back to blame me for action I took as a child, I doubt I would have behaved differently. Visibly shaken and off center, Denise tried hard to be decent and keep a good face for everyone. I was the outsider. I could plainly see the reality of an extremely dysfunctional family.

The weekend ended without too much drama and Denise took off, seeing her mother for the last time. She would not return for the funeral. I didn't blame her.

A week or so later, when Dolores thought she wanted to go ahead and get the dying in motion, she stopped eating for three days and laid in the dark of her hospital room. When death did not come on command, we arrived the next day to see her sitting in her bed, blinds open, freshly showered, hair styled and eating a burger! Apparently, she had changed her mind. "I'm hungry," De said and happily chomped on her hamburger as if she had a new lease on life. We were stunned.

The next day, she took several blood transfusions, buying almost two more months of a torturous existence for everyone concerned.

One evening, after we stopped to visit before heading out to dinner for my birthday, she seemed angry as the nurses streamed into her hospital room to offer catcalls over my lovely dress, clothes and heels. Dolores was miffed and did not like the air of excitement in the room, or attention on anyone except herself. We made a quick exit and headed out to dinner.

Since I knew her only a mere bit beyond formality, it seemed odd to me that she frequently burped her colostomy bag in our presence without so much as a warning glance. It had to be her distaste for her son and not me, I thought, as I was doing everything I could to make her comfortable and get to know her in the little time she had left. Those incidents turned my stomach and left me gagging and choking, as her brutal lack of concern for offending anyone in her room with the noxious stench of shit and gas from the bag leaked out and smothered us until we could spray the air and open windows.

What exactly does the public burping of a colostomy bag mean? What does shit represent in this picture? Knowing her history as an actress and theatrical bent, I don't doubt it was her own personal joke. Dolores was a money fanatic, as portrayed by notes all over the house, recording every cent she spent, jars of money, stocks and bonds. She had a razor-sharp intellect, but she was completely deranged. She had gone after her daughter with a butcher knife. Simultaneously, she was a local actress who had starred in numerous plays. Bizarre mix of talent and crazy.

Exactly one year earlier, I had been on a beach in Cape Cod with my family and grandmother. I could not help but reflect, comparing the two women. We cooked spaghetti, laughed and enjoyed the picturesque view from our deck. Nobody was mean, although loud yelling and meddling in each other's business are an acceptable part of Italian family culture; nobody would have called it unusual or took offense.

Six weeks later, life changed in a moment's notice with a tragic accident involving my mother, my grandmother and a Jeep. I thought back to her peaceful and graceful exit and compared it to this one. Ida was so kind and peaceful as she lay dying, accepting her fate and unwilling to create anymore distress on her beloved family than knowing we would suffer for her going. When the time came for her post-surgery physical rehab, she gently refused and told me directly that she had no interest in going on, when I reprimanded her for not taking her sessions with her therapist.

Ida knew the inactivity would lead to pneumonia, but she was ready to go and did not change her mind. A stroke ended her life within two weeks, and she died after two days day of quiet and peaceful shallow breathing. She held my hand until I let go of hers.

I could not help but compare the two experiences. Both women were in their eighties and both had bladder cancer. Other than that, I could not see any similarities.

Old sentiments die hard in families. Dolores constantly reminded her son that if displeased with him at any moment, her trust was revocable; that if he even slightly displeased her, the pot at the end of the rainbow could disappear as quickly as his thoughts of the anticipated riches arose.

One night, when she felt anger for some reason we did not know, she told him in no uncertain terms how she felt. "I cannot believe I gave birth to something like you," she spat. It was difficult to comprehend a mother speaking such a thing to her son, but perhaps she had her own reasons.

Looking back, she was being honest and knew him far better than I, but at that moment, I was stunned by her cruelty in the face of his doing everything possible to act accordingly with her wishes during the final weeks of her life. She spared no insult, often finding words so harsh, nobody deserved them.

She came home briefly, and we shared around-the-clock shifts with nurses. Her lucidity was fair in the beginning, but as multiple ailments began to shut her body down, breathing became difficult. Her doctor prescribed Ativan to help her remain clam.

The care her doctors and nurses displayed showed deep concern for her humanity and dignity; I thought she missed it completely since she showed no form of gratitude for the genuine concern and kindness several of our care providers and her family showed. Death can be a slow process, especially in the case of chronic illness. In this case, it would take the remainder of my first summer in Sitka. Brian and I worked remarkably well as a team to support each other.

When Dolores insulted her Filipino nurse and me when we tried to talk or offer her options, it was apparent that she was sliding mentally, and the cocktail of drugs didn't help. She began to hallucinate, we thought, but according to her doctor, may actually have been revisiting times in her past, from many years ago.

The one day I cared for her each week drained me. Brian couldn't cope with her needs and behaviors. One evening, close to midnight, as we approached the eve of her death, we received a call from the nurse on duty. We had gone home to rest, and the nurse was in a panic.

It was a struggle to get Dolores to use her diapers to urinate. She was a tall, large-boned woman who insisted on hauling herself out of bed to use her bathroom, but once up, could not get there without help. She threw her body over the rails of the hospital bed we had brought home and insisted we take her to her bathroom. It was unimaginable to me that a woman of her size and her condition could have so much physical strength at this moment.

When we arrived, she had wrapped and tangled her lone oxygen line around her hands, arms and wrists and refused to unravel it. She was unable to explain why she had done it, but after some gentle discussion with me, I was able to get her to allow me to disentangle the line from around her hands. It was the end of July and death rapidly approached. She sank daily, to the point that we couldn't cope with the demands. She lost a lot of blood and became delusional about being kept prisoner, wanting to make phone calls and use her computer, all of which were out of the question given her rapidly deteriorating physical and mental condition.

At age 84, Dolores was a force. Just two months earlier, she still managed her own needs and business. Her ability to invest and manage money was admirable. She had turned a modest income over her lifetime and a minor education in business into an estate worth over $5 million.

CHAPTER 10

Time for Death and Drama

"Dying is easy, it's living that scares me to death."
—*Annie Lennox*

IT WAS AUGUST when Dolores returned to the hospital. The doc agreed it was time and we realized we had misunderstood the Medicare regulations—we had to admit her back to the hospital at this particular time if we wanted insurance to pay for the stay. Since De stated she "could not afford" her nurses, we agreed it was the best choice.

The doctor repeatedly suggested we bring in a "massage therapist". We did not understand, but as it turned out, this person was an energy worker, who, with crystals and some time alone in Dolores's room, helped her to let go. She placed rose crystals and other items throughout her room, in order to calm the angry energy that was palpable upon entry.

Dolores would die days later, while gripping the handrails of the bed, resisting death fiercely, in her anger as it tried its best to claim her. Her faith apparently offered little comfort as she moved toward death. She refused to tell her son she loved him, despite his telling her that several times in her last weeks of life. She simply could not or would not give him that peace in her dying. I guess she figured the money was enough.

Not once did I hear a word of God mentioned by her or any sign that her lifelong membership in her church or her faith in God and a better place offered solace. Once, after members of her church visited her for prayer, I watched for some sign of acceptance, peace or solace in her demeanor, but found none.

I visited her alone, on the night prior to her death, close to midnight. She was unresponsive but still gripping the bed rails. I quietly told her it was "okay to go." That I would care for Denise and Brian, and that she did not have to worry about them. The room was quiet. I knew she would pass very soon and reported this to Brian, as he was unable emotionally to visit her that evening.

At noon the following day, I was at my part-time job at the local art gallery, which I had gotten my very first week in town. It was important to me to retain some independence and I enjoyed meeting the tourists who visited Sitka daily. I even knew a few who came in from New York.

My phone rang, and I could barely hear Brian's voice, which was a first. His mother had passed.

The cruise season was winding down. I called my boss and closed the store.

I was the first to arrive at the hospital though Allison and Brian were already supposed to be there. I suspected they had polished one or two drinks off first. When Allison saw her dead grandmother, the poor thing burst into tears. Seeing someone dead is a shock to anyone. We hugged. It was over.

The three of us stayed less than ten minutes. In contrast, a year earlier, none of our family could bring ourselves to leave my grandmother's hospital room after she died. We stayed with her for hours.

People react differently to death. I went back to work. Brian and Allison went home. Soon after, Allison went to her friend's house. I didn't want my love to be alone. I got permission to close the shop and headed home within the hour to find Brian quietly seated on the couch. He had lit several candles. It was something to do with "keeping her spirit out". The silence was deafening and not at all peaceful. We talked briefly and decided to go over to the Pioneer Bar and have a Guinness to celebrate Dolores's life in the Irish tradition.

Brian, on an empty stomach, got drunk and went to bed after we came home. I cooked pasta, as it was the only thing I knew to do. Italians offer ample helpings of food at times of both grief and happiness. Food fixes all. No matter the event, food is always a key aspect of any life event for an Italian woman and the ultimate expression of love.

Brian left his cell phone on the kitchen counter, face up.

While I was cooking, a message popped up on his phone from a woman. I tracked their sexting all the way back to the weekend I had arrived in Sitka. Of course, no mention of his engagement. Utter shock threatened to knock me over.

My heart caved in. I decided not to respond at that moment. She had texted a sexual fantasy of fucking him on a church altar and had sent pictures of her bare breasts.

It was a quiet evening, and I washed the dishes, shaking with anger and disbelief as Allison heartily finished dinner, never offering to assist in cleanup. After she departed, I was left alone to wonder how I would handle her father's betrayal.

The flurry of post-death haste began the next day. Monday morning, things started moving fast. We visited the funeral home and made arrangements for the service to take place one week later, after Dolores had been sent to Ketchikan for cremation and her ashes were returned to Sitka. My best friend was on the ferry with my car, due to arrive that day, having traveled from Florida to Alaska to drive it up to me. Brian's son was coming from Anchorage and in a surprise twist, his stepbrother was also en route from South Carolina. Brian was concerned about his motivation for the trip. The two had never been close, and Brian wondered if his stepbrother was after money.

It turned out that after some conversation, all he had wanted to do was request a few items be returned to him as they had belonged to his father, Dolores's second husband. Dolores did not mention him in her will, nor did she leave him anything.

We located the obituary and edited it as needed, working hard to dig out old photos for the memory board.

Helen arrived first, and I almost knocked her down with my bear hug.

Seeing the ferry come into Sitka and knowing she was on it had comforted me instantly. "I am exhausted," she claimed, "but it was the trip of a lifetime!" The wide array of characters she had met on the trip exchanged stories and plans for a new life in Alaska. People making the move to the Last Frontier are looking for awe. Alaska never disappoints.

Brian began to show signs of wear. I learned I could bear quite a bit more frustration, discomfort and inconvenience than I would have thought possible. Unfamiliar personalities, mixing for the first time around a funeral, lend themselves to unusual and spontaneous conversations as the unrelated parties attempt to get to know one another in the circumstance of loss they unwittingly share. Tempers flared.

In creating the board of photos seen at so many memorial services, Allison had neglected to include any photos of her brother and his grandmother. I pointed this out and Brian unleashed fury on me, as if I had something to do with this mishap. He refused to speak with Allison about including her brother. I eventually found a photo or two and set them on the table in front of the board.

My new reality: Innocent mistakes were unforgivable crimes.

Crying, after being ridiculed for asking to buy an appropriate dress for the funeral and for "criticizing" his perfect daughter and her artistic creation, I broke down for the first time since my arrival in Sitka. "You always have to look good. Why can't you just *be* good?" This was the first round of many harsh words; arisen I now believe as a result of a misunderstand of cultural differences and his complete intolerance for anything he didn't deem important.

I sat in the car in the driveway in tears. Brian realized he had erred and said, "It does not have to be over." Apparently, he had been here before. The sobbing. The exit thereafter.

I threw the money for the dress back at him, choosing to wear an ill-fitting suit instead. The money rained down on the floor of the passenger's side of the car and landed like litter on a sidewalk in New York City. He was contrite for the remainder of the day. Hurt as I was, I attributed it all to the impending funeral and grief.

Earlier that day, after opening my bedside table drawer for the first time, I discovered previously used sex toys left behind from prior women. He was angry with me and refused to acknowledge my discomfort at the sight of them, shouting "My mother died! I don't have time for your drama." His sex toys were somehow my drama. Minimization like this and insults capped every hour. I didn't know how I would get through this day.

Looking back, I probably seemed so foreign to them. A New Yorker in Alaska. My East Coast reputation preceded me, and my manners and sense of propriety must have seemed so snotty given the casual manners and lack of consideration I was beginning to notice. The refinement and direct communication that does not leave much to doubt in New York was just not necessary in Sitka, where most communication was indirect. You had to pay close attention to the words that weren't spoken to decipher the fucking meaning of the message.

Dolores, freshly reduced to ash, had arrived back in town to be buried in the church altar with her daughter at St. Peter's. I mostly stayed out of this, as my own history of religious abuse often reared its ugly head when organized religion attempted to enter my life on any level. A child of a converted Jehovah's Witness, I had had my fill of forced beliefs and shuddered at any involvement around the religious aspect of things. It was just too much trauma.

We ordered magnificent flowers and obtained permission to have them in the church only to be told later it was against the rules of the Episcopal Church to have flowers. I guess hearing that Dolores had left the largest bequeath in church history, persuaded them to change their minds.

It's amazing what $500,000 will do. "The flowers are in," Father Dave said, and it was done.

Prior to the conclusion of the service and her grandmother's burial, Allison departed. After all, she had a softball game that day.

Once again, appalled at the lack of manners I saw, I remarked to Brian how badly her selfish behavior reflected on the family. Unable to stand up to her because of his own guilt, shame and fear of her abandoning him, he passed it off as "just fine." His past behaviors and abuse prevented him from taking any stand. She would use it against him, and she had learned the art of manipulation from a pro. The service was appropriate and well attended. A few former mayors and town icons showed up, including Dolores's older lady friends and a smattering of church members. Some, who we thought would be there, were not; others we did not consider, showed up. I could have behaved better, refusing to shake hands and say "Peace be with you" as they do in this sort of service.

It made my skin crawl, and I could not force myself to participate, thereby offending at least one parishioner who did not understand my refusal to shake her hand. My trauma from childhood religious abuse was another form of PTSD, and I was extremely uncomfortable while trying to be supportive of my fiancée.

Then family posed for photos in the church, a funeral practice I had not seen before.

CHAPTER 11

Ghastly Legacy

*"Let parents bequeath to their children not
riches, but the spirit of reverence."*

—*Plato*

BRIAN AND HIS sister, Denise, were the sole heirs to $5 million.
Neither ever had access to amounts of money like this or had even
thought of what they would do with an amount more than survival
funds. The anticipation of the inheritance was not much help in
making it feel real.

For anyone who has inherited money suddenly, there is a certain
amount of shock that must wear off after the money is deposited
in one's hand. It is almost incomprehensible to have sudden freedom; choices never before present to make. If combined, as in this
case, with a long and solid history of substance abuse, things can get
messy quickly.

The oceanfront home was lovely, and the renovations began
immediately after the estate was settled in March of 2015, after a great
deal of wrangling with the law firm who drew the trust and Brian's
struggle to understand complex legal matters that nobody explained.

In my opinion, the firm bilked both mother and son by capitalizing on their lack of legal experience through unnecessary and complicated legal arrangements in a state where few laws get in the way of people's plans. The state, having no inheritance tax, combined with falling just under federal inheritance tax amounts, should have been simple. Instead, it took well over seven months and the combined efforts of a CPA and the law firm to "approve" the release of funds to the heirs.

Any mention of my concerns to my then fiancée resulted in anger and fits of temper directed at me in such a way that I just stopped responding. Even if he asked for my opinion, he criticized it, although I might be in agreement with him. He truly was a mystery.

Brian was the sole trustee responsible for the management and administration of his sister's money. He admittedly gave her enough funds to provide for comfortable living space and to kill herself with alcohol.

Until the inheritance, she lived in a rooming house and slept with her tattered mattress on the floor, surrounded by filthy ashtrays overflowing with cigarette ash. We visited her several times in Everett, Washington to locate new living arrangements, buying furniture and essential items for basic comfort. A visit two months later showed boxes never opened and trash piled up in the kitchen of her brand-new apartment.

After a trip to Best Buy, and over $2000 later, Brian generously purchased a pair of Bose headphones for me, from Denise's trust fund, asking me, "What color do you want? She will never notice." I was too appalled to even respond. If I had challenged the morality of his decision, especially in Best Buy, he would have lost his temper. A working real estate appraiser, she chain-smoked and drove a car held together with spit and putty, cigarette ashes flying in the wind as she steered the rickety automobile. We purchased a new Jeep on that trip, too.

Denise survived a bout with breast cancer and her skin had a gray-green tinge of poor health and bad nutrition. A photo of her in her mother's credenza bore no resemblance as I asked who that person was in the photo. I was terribly embarrassed.

Bad dentures prevented her from eating much. At dinner that weekend, she consumed three fishbowl glasses of wine before her salad arrived. It distressed me to watch her try and chew. Her discomfort from the ill-fitting dentures was evident and mostly she drank, choosing to eat her salad in the backseat of the car, with her hands as we drove her home, shouting directions to her apartment between bites. Dolores directed that her daughter be given a comfortable home, with good furniture and a new car. Health insurance allowed her to treat her various ailments from a post-cancer bout and get some much-needed comforts. She specifically used the term "generous" when she described the care her brother was to provide for her. No matter the money, she was on a slow road to death from substance abuse and nothing anyone did would change her direction now. She would be gone in less than five years, leaving Brian with full control and all the money. When I got news of her passing in June of 2020, it was with great sadness. We had forged a nice friendship and I even helped her take legal action against Brian for conning her out of a large sum of her inheritance. Revenge can be sweet.

We suggested Denise visit the salon and get a good haircut and pedicure, but she, at age 60, never having had one, insisted that nobody was going to touch her feet.

Brian did his best to follow his mother's directive, but Denise did not make it easy. Likeable enough with a loud voice and a boisterous sense of humor, she had been living life alone, with no family, children or any husband to look after her. Her job provided the bare minimum, but it appeared to be a very rough existence. There was no evidence of friends.

Lacking even basic social graces, she did not seem to notice that pauses in conversation were part of conversation and her brother's already thin patience was adding to the tension as she shouted driving directions from the backseat, competing with our GPS system.

The money must have been a shock to her, too. Nether of the heirs knew until just prior to Dolores's death the actual value of the estate. Since it was under the ceiling for federal inheritance tax and Alaska having no such tax, the money was free and clear. Although Brian tried to explain it, Denise kept asking the same questions. It was as if each of us had to keep hearing the words to make it real.

"Five million dollars," he repeated. "Five million dollars."

Until a man finds himself, it is said he will ruin every woman he comes across. Brian, too, had his share of shock. Cozy in the Music Projects suite at the Alexis Hotel in Seattle again, with a stellar view of the Great Wheel and Puget Sound, he offered a rare moment of insight. "I am so unhappy, and I don't know why," he said. "I have all of this money and a loving partner, and I am so unhappy."

"Brian, please do what you need to, to take care of yourself," I responded. "You have not taken any time in your life to find out what makes you happy. If you need to go away for a while, if you need to be alone, I will be here when you get back. Go find what matters to you."

Finally, faced with choices that could be whatever his heart desired, Brian realized he had no idea who he was and had no idea what to do next. I saw it all unfolding and felt helpless and frightened to risk his anger by saying too much.

I reminded him that no matter how mean-spirited she had been, Dolores could have left her fortune to anyone she chose to. With generous donations to her church and her community library, Dolores chose to leave the majority of her fortune to her children and that said more than any word she could have spoken. She possessed a thread of decency, as confusing as it was.

CHAPTER 12

Catcalls from Wife Material

"If you want something said, ask a man; if you want something done, ask a woman."

—*Margaret Thatcher*

HAVING TRADED MY five-inch open-toed heels and suits for black leggings and Xtratuf brown rubber boots, which I would not have worn to work in my yard in New York but are the height of fashion in Sitka, I got used to them, at least for everyday life. Call me crazy, but these boots became as symbolic as bears during my time in Alaska. They resembled strength, sturdiness, conquering. Walking down Katlian Street, which runs through the center of town and through the fish processing plants on the harbor, eight out of ten people will be wearing them at any given time. I've seen entire families marching down the street, all decked out in brown rubber boots. Women wear them to concerts and with dresses. (That's a bit too far, in my opinion, but I experimented a few times like a maniacal wildlife stylist!)

Alaskan women loved my heels though. I got overzealous catcalls from women, not men, as I crossed the street downtown.

"I love your shoes!" a woman shouted at me, as I walked to the art gallery one day. This was directed at a pair of heels nobody would have taken a second look at back east.

Guns are also important to the collective women's narrative in Alaska. For a quick show of an Alaska driver's license, you could walk out with a glossy 9 mm 45 Glock like I did. No permits, classes or fingerprints!

Being thin is not required in Alaska, and it sounded like as good a reason as any to justify the extra ten I gained since moving there. Women are valued by how practical they are. Many have professional fishing careers that began as deck hands. These women love the outdoor life, and many have made their fortunes by it. Some are married to crusty and hardworking bearded fishermen, a few of whom are fortunate and wealthy, owning huge boats that bring in catches that support generations and build fortunes.

Can women set a skate? Not an ice skate, but the kind used to pull in halibut or salmon catches as allowed by law. It's called a SHARC permit, and it allows every Alaska resident to provide food for their families. According to the application, you're allowed fifteen halibut per day. Subsistence is a way of life in Alaska, a place so harsh and unforgiving, yet abundant in food sources. One day's halibut catch was worth close to $3,000. I didn't even like halibut but tried a few times to amass a horde of it.

Alaskan women have a funny sense of humor. A friend mailed a fishing permit application to me after being a guest on her boat of a local couple for a day of whale watching. Once she learned I had been in the state for a year, she told me to apply, but cautioned me that my boyfriend would have to watch me work from inside the boat.

As I pulled in the skate, my French manicure remained intact!

As other women marveled at me, this small, remote fishing village seduced me slowly. Everyone seemed to live in Sitka because they valued individuality, and many were very opinionated. They were crazy nature lovers also, and nature never disappointed.

Expectations were not so present and simplicity, necessitated by few choices, ruled. Individuality truly shaped this place, as the local characters added rich flavor to this small, tight-knit community. It wasn't so much a choice of where to go for dinner but more about which place happened to be open that given evening in the off season, or in summer, and which place was not filled with reservations from out-of-towners.

Locals are not given much extra consideration. The lack of competition keeps prices high and customer service low. A nail appointment is booked three months out. Having what you want, when you want it, doesn't exist in Sitka.

And thank heavens for Amazon Prime, but even with this service that now dominates the planet, some distributors didn't ship to Alaska under any circumstance. The state *is* part of the United States, you know!

On one occasion, after a lot of catcalls, while getting a manicure, I smelled something fishy. The young woman next to me realized I was puzzled and proceeded to describe her trek to town by boat that day. She lived on a small island ten minutes off of Sitka and took her boat into town. While in reverse, she almost hit a whale and was sprayed when the whale took a breath, clouding her in a smelly, fishy mist. This was a typical interaction with other women in Sitka.

CHAPTER 13

Profile of an Abuser

"Above all, don't lie to yourself. The man who lies to himself and listens to his own lie comes to a point where he cannot distinguish the truth within him or around him, so he loses respect for himself. And having no respect, he ceases to love."
—*Fyodor Dostoevsky*

HELEN'S PRESENCE DURING that rough period after Dolores's death certainly helped balance the tension and grief, as she made her usual crude jokes, cooked and cleaned. She overstayed on my behalf. I showed her some of the ways of Alaskan women. She heard the cat-calls, too!

The contrast between Helen and Brian's step-brother was striking and at times, hilarious. Adding my future stepson to the mix was even funnier. A right-wing Christian and a Jehovah's Witness in the same room made for interesting conversation. For once, I decided not to offer my opinion each time he offended me and my core beliefs with discussion about things such as "mandatory vaccination" and a god I did not identify with.

Obviously, my level of frustration simmered underneath the surface since the evening I saw the sext message on Brian's phone about fucking on the church altar, but it would be two weeks before I could properly address it.

When Helen left, I cried my heart out. On the same day, as if on cue, another email showed up from a woman called TP, who had been engaging in daily correspondence with Brian. In the flurry of words, I didn't see my name once.

It was time. Fueled by sadness over Helen leaving and sheer anger that had been building, that evening, the tension exploded. Brian's own hypervigilance kept him in immediate tune with the slightest change in my energy. I told him we had a problem we needed to resolve and confronted him about the first sext message and now this email.

I remained calm, watching his reactions as I explained the concern and stated, "This is not the kind of relationship I want. It is not why I came here. If this is what you want, I need to go." I began to reveal my recent discoveries.

He immediately responded, admitting he was not sure I was here to stay and that he has always kept a "Plan B". He promised to stop the communications and for a while, he did. But I never trusted him again.

I observed him entering his passwords and monitored his email and texts going forward. Hypervigilance became a way of daily life for me, too.

Summer wound down in Sitka. Events mark the change of season, as the weather does not vary much in temperature. Millions of salmon begin their run home to spawn and die. The rivers swell and stink with rotting fish. The days grow shorter. The last of the cruise ships depart and businesses open all summer begin to close down. When the Channel Club and Ludvig's, two fine dining establishments in Sitka, close, it's officially the "off "season. I dreaded it because we had so few choices to begin with. Losing the top two for six months felt oppressive when combined with the impending darkness. There are not many distractions and people tend to turn toward alcohol, spending nights in the Pioneer Bar, drinking cheap whiskey and beer, smoking still allowed.

The stark contrast between the shortest days of the year with five hours of sunlight versus the longest, with about twenty-three hours, in this part of the world, is striking. As summer vanishes, the minutes disappear rapidly as darkness overwhelms the quiet town. Folks leave town for warm dry sun and tropical destinations and the town becomes sleepy as the rains roll in during October.

I couldn't help but think of the horror film, "30 Days of Night", focusing on an Alaskan town beset by vampires as it enters into a thirty-day long polar night.

Rhythms change and people stay indoors more, resting, cooking and enjoying the fish catches of summer, along with many of the canned and frozen salmon and blueberries harvested from lush low bushes found in abundance during the summer months. Even the bears, with berry bushes stripped by eager harvesters and without salmon, mostly turn in and sleep.

Finally, spring arrives again, and with it, the herring season opens. Fifty or so boats come to town. Thousands of tons of the fish quotas are caught and processed as the excitement of residents and fishermen combine to ring in the season. Wildlife is abundant as the food supply increases. The bears wake and begin to move around.

In September, we flew to Anchorage for a business trip. With a population of about 300,000 people, Anchorage is Alaska's bustling city. There is even a spa and a mall, including a Nordstrom…woohoo! It was heaven, and as state residents, we were allowed three free bags on Alaska Airlines, when traveling in state. Again, most Alaskans have to get on a plane just to buy a lipstick.

You can also drive out of Anchorage to many destinations. Nine hundred miles and a two-hour flight north of Sitka, it's colder, darker and drier than the Southeast. Brian's son, Walter, and ex-wife also live there, and we were fortunate enough to be in town to celebrate his son's birthday.

Not long after the candles were blown out, after seeing a movie about a family in theatres, I casually remarked to Brian how much I missed my own family. This unleashed such a fury in him, I was barely able to drive to Costco, where I inadvertently cut off another driver vying for my parking spot.

She got out of her car and began shouting at me. I apologized as best I could, while he jumped out to go shop, asking me if I would be here when he came out.

"Every fucking day," he shouted at me. "Every fucking day, you complain and whine about this!" His intolerance was magnificent, shining brightly for me to see. I was in such a state of shock, rankled and so physically shaken by the volume of his shouting, I could barely think. It took several hours for me to calm myself, trying hard not think about what had just happened.

I had never been spoken to like this. I played it like Scarlett O'Hara and thought, *I won't think about this now, I'll think about it tomorrow.* It was not my best plan.

How many times do we brush this kind of treatment off, take the weight of it out, until it's a hollow "mistake" that we invent a dozen reasons for? We don't want to see it for what it is: Wrong. Warning sign. Oscar Wilde said, "Never love anyone who treats you like you're ordinary." But even ordinary, which I never considered myself to be, didn't deserve this.

In her book, *The Sociopath Next Door*, Martha Stout describes characteristics of a sociopath, claiming that they make up about 4% of the population and possess at least three of the following seven traits: 1) failure to conform to social norms; (2) deceitful-ness, manipulative-ness; (3) impulsivity, failure to plan ahead; (4) irritability, aggressiveness; (5) reckless disregard for safety of self or others; (6) consistent irresponsibility; (7) lack of remorse after having hurt, mistreated or stolen from another person, and always,

always a refusal to accept responsibility for their own actions. The presence of any three of these "symptoms" is enough to make many psychiatrists suspect the disorder.

If I had taken the time to think, I would have to do something, like maybe LEAVE, but that was too much to process in the moment.

We had a wedding to attend in New York in two weeks. In my fantasy mind, things could not fall apart now. I loved him, yet I could not rationalize his anger, insults and intolerance. Brian's behaviors left me disoriented, as he so often told me how much he loved me. There was a stunning contrast between words and actions. I saved an email that he had written to me prior to my move to Sitka.

> I am just heading off to bed but wanted to write you before I did. I have so many things to thank you for. My lasting impression of the last couple of days is you with your hat cocked at a jaunty angle, with your smile and your eyes. Those eyes that when I look in them, ask a question and also answer questions without even trying.
>
> I love you. You are to me the love I have been looking for. I can see it in your eyes. They are true. They show me what you feel inside. I am so grateful for you Adriana. You have no idea. Allison had something funny to say tonight. I was telling her about Eataly.
>
> We were having sausage and cheese and I was saying how you could get anything Italian there. She looked at me and said, "Even an Italian wife?" I just smiled at her and raised my eyebrows. So, I hope that makes you smile as it did me. I am so thankful for you, my dear. I love you more than words can capture.
>
> I hope your Monday is full of happiness and joy.
>
> Brian

Pay close attention; between the public scorn and the charming correspondence, this is a profile of an abuser, I would learn. Violence escalates over time, gradually getting worse and moving from slight insults to full-on tantrums and then physical altercation. I did not have this information quite yet.

The especially disturbing feature of this relationship was his wild swing from love to hate, back to love and then hate again. It was a full thirty-day cycle when after weeks of tension, he would lose his temper, blame me for everything, tell me how I felt (really, how *he* felt), and then he would turn the whole thing around on me. Eventually, I would come to learn that abuse does have a cycle and if you know this, it's an easy one to recognize. Each time, he created a scenario where he played both judge and jury, and I was guilty every time.

Ignoring me, choosing to read his iPad for hours and a lack of sexual attention and affection, in general, when angry with me could go on for as long as two weeks. He would just act as if I were not there.

After he unleashed his anger on me, his behavior would turn towards cooperative, pleasant and temperate for a couple of weeks before the tension began to mount once again.

Looking back, I can see that stating any personal preference or disagreement with how he did anything all was grounds for his temper and vitriol to be released on me. Any small demonstration of need I might express for even basic emotional support as I adjusted to my new home was met with fury and verbal abuse. In moments that I asked for a simple shoulder to cry on, his anger was even worse. He would become furious for me for any need I might demonstrate. This is known as a technique called "gas lighting" a person's character.

Playing with another's memory and then telling them they don't remember events creates instability and makes one doubt their own recall. I began to feel crazy and stupid as Brian told me I could not remember things he had obviously already told me multiple times.

Stout, in *The Sociopath Next Door*, explains that sociopaths as a group have documented characteristics. One or more of the frequently observed traits is a glib and superficial charm that allows the sociopath to seduce other people, figuratively or literally—a kind of glow or charisma that at least initially can make the sociopath seem more interesting or charming than most of the normal people around him.

As a group, they are known, according to Stout, for their pathological lying and conning. They may also have a history of early behavior problems, sometimes including drug use and always including a failure to acknowledge responsibility for any problems that occurred.

People talk about gaslighting and other features that should kill any fantasies of building a life with that person much more frequently today than they did even five years ago. Unfortunately, I slipped through the cracks of this knowledge at the time. Even so, I still thought Brian was husband material! What does that say about me?

CHAPTER 14

Torn Between

"Action cures fear. Indecision, postponement,
on the other hand, fertilize fear."
—David Walter Schwartz

THE WEDDING IN New York was fun, with no major disturbance or disagreement. We traveled separately. I arrived a week prior to Brian and stayed a week later, as he refused to take more time off from work to learn more about the woman he was to marry and where she came from.

Brian had never been to the East Coast, much less an Italian wedding, and the amount of food was a big surprise to him, although it was a modest wedding by East Coast standards. We had the standard fare of beef, chicken, fish and lots of farmed shrimp cocktail from Vietnam; something Brian found hysterical, asking why people were lined up at that table. I was not sure what he meant, but as he explained that in Alaska, people don't eat shrimp like that, I began to understand.

We were fish snobs in Alaska. King salmon rules and the wild shrimp tastes just like king crab. Wild-caught halibut is abundant, and diets are rich in fish and fresh seafood. Live king crab arrives at the harbor in early spring and it's a feast fit for a king. Alaska natives also hunt seal and sea otter for meat and fur, but non-natives are prohibited from doing so.

One day, we stopped at my storage unit, selecting ten boxes of my personal things to ship north. While we were there, Brian said the rest would take a "couple of years", since we did not have the room for my things. When I questioned him, he said my art was not Alaskan and it did not "fit" the décor. He then informed me that I would have to pay for half of the bill for shipping in order to demonstrate "skin in the game" of our relationship.

Looking back, the comment was unacceptable. I should have ended it right there. I was more than willing to pay half, but the way he said it implied that my moving all the way to Alaska (and taking care of his dying mother, I might add), was not enough, and that his meeting my family meant nothing. I thought my move alone showed just how much precious skin I did have in the fucking game!

It was difficult to make sense of that statement and I wrestled with it for months, never coming to terms with it or finding any measure of comfort no matter how I moved the words around in my head.

It was abusive, plain and simple. It strikes me that when we are abused, we don't want to see it. We are busy making sure we are right, and we don't want to acknowledge how wrong some things are. After all, that realization could—and should—change everything.

I returned to Alaska in time for the major state holiday, Alaska Day, which is celebrated in a big way in Sitka. Alaska Day commemorates the day the United States purchased Alaska from Russia. It's a day of parades and festivities, pie eating and visiting with friends, as locals usher in fall rains and the arrival of the season. Brian asked that I be home in time to share the day with him, and although it held no real interest for me and I despise parades, I honored his request.

It wasn't the bonding experience that I had fantasized about after being apart, but I tried to get lost in the original live music by Gaaja

Heen dancers, the New Archangel Dancers, the U.S. Army Band, and the Seattle Fire Pipes & Drums.

Christmas came. It was a quiet day, with our kids in Anchorage and New York. We cooked a delicious duck dinner together and had only one visitor.

Mark, Brian's one "good friend" and a heavy drug user stopped by. When he offered to get high, Brian said "sure" as he looked over me. When he saw the expression of displeasure on my face, he thought better of it.

There is a kind of lethargy, a fatigue so great that set in that first year. By the end of December, we were feeling exhausted from the lack of light and we planned a trip to Palm Springs to soak up a little sun. Brian made all the choices about where we would go and stay.

Things were gradually worsening at home. Every day, I went to work at the hospital, my second job, making sure to tell my office mate and co-workers about the happenings at home. In case anything happened to me, I wanted evidence that I had informed others about the slow escalation toward violence. Even having a thought like this is a hint abuse is taking place. Healthy relationships have no such components.

"He is going to kill you," my co-worker said. "If you want to pack boxes and leave, I will help you. I have a truck, and you can store boxes at my place."

I couldn't quite conceive this. But it's like I was split in two, between what I knew as plain reality—after all, going through the motions of telling a coworker everything so someone else "knew" of the danger I might be in—and idealizing my perfect husband material.

I held onto hope that things would improve, coming close to canceling the trip to Palm Springs and breaking off the engagement, but I attributed so much of his anger toward his unresolved grief over the death of his mother four months earlier. Once he had time to heal, I thought, things would be normal again.

In men, depression often manifests as anger. I gave him the benefit of the doubt and buckled down, trying to be tough, reigning in my boundaries when I felt he was becoming abusive while understanding at the same time. I was becoming increasingly lonely and anxious as I realized I could not verbalize any feelings or need for emotional support. It was too risky. Eggshells I walked on could easily shatter.

Our time in Palm Springs went well. There were no major disturbances (a disjointed measure for the quality of life we should seek and demand), and we enjoyed a week in the sun, dining and shopping and lounging poolside, complimentary champagne flowing courtesy of the owners of the Palm Springs Hotel. It was a newly renovated boutique property, and we were among the first guests to arrive. Our host and his wife were gracious, and the lodging was comfortable and modern with fireplaces poolside, rooms decorated with portraits of celebrities like James Dean and Marilyn Monroe.

It takes a few days of sunshine to offset the sluggishness caused by a lack of light, but by the third day, we felt human once again as the energy from the sun recharged our batteries and brightened our spirits. We fantasized about living in Palm Springs. We even visited a few open houses to check out the real estate offerings.

We landed a week later on Baranof Island in darkness and rain. I began to cry silently at the contrast to the bright and beautiful sunshine we had left behind, and Brian showed me a rare kindness by acknowledging he understood how I felt and said he felt the same way. Once again, he sensed my mood without ever looking my way. In those moments, I felt a shard of light pierce my fears and give me hope for our future. I looked hard and hoped daily for signs like this one. They were few and far between.

CHAPTER 15

Shock and Awe

"Expect nothing. Live frugally by surprise."
—*Alice Walker*

BACK AT WORK on Monday, I saw an ad posted for a corporate recruiter in the hospital where I worked. Earning a tiny hourly wage and working far below my education and past experience, I applied and pursued the opportunity that paid $20,000 more. I landed the job and was to begin a few weeks later. A grand flower arrangement arrived, courtesy of Brian.

Brian often visited me for lunch at work where we ate in the cafeteria. I think he came for appearances, as he left after a brief lunch to rush home and enjoy his time alone. When I came home after work and shared my day, he got incensed and said I was not to discuss work after I left it.

February rolled into March and we took a weekend trip to Seattle to visit the family. We looked for an apartment for Denise and signed a lease, buying furniture and other items she would need to live with more comfort than she had available in her recent past. I enjoyed the frequent travel, and it broke the routine and darkness up a bit. In late March, after a brief trip to Juneau, we knew Brian had to visit Denise in Washington again to retrieve her signature on important trust papers. We could not trust her to sign and return them by mail, as she was just too unpredictable.

Prior to the trip, I discovered four pairs of women's panties in my fiancé's sock drawer while putting clean laundry away. I had not noticed them previously, and his words were something like, "You are not as smart as you think you are. They have been in that drawer the entire time." His explanation was neither plausible nor acceptable. A stack of foreign panties had not been in that drawer even a few days earlier.

His final statement and explanation to my questions about why he had kept the panties knowing how much it would hurt me was that he felt "defiant".

I tried to give Brian possible explanations and he rejected them out of hand. He had once said casually, "You can tell a liar if they change their story." He knew I knew this and so he refused to discuss any plausible reason for the panties. There was none! Three weeks after Valentine's Day, one pair of panties audaciously displayed red and pink hearts all over them.

All the same size, but with missing labels and tags, Brian insisted they were from different women. "One woman took them off in the ladies' room at a dinner date and stuffed them in my blazer pocket," he said.

I had no idea what was going on and decided to remain calm, observe and make a phone call. I needed answers and was shaken to my core. I immediately phoned his ex-wife and we spoke about their past. She explained that he had cheated on her and had been violent. She said she thought he had "learned his lesson" from past consequences, but hearing my story, she realized he had not. I asked her if she thought he would kill me. "No," she said flatly.

I had met her and her husband a year earlier when they were in Sitka for a month on business, and the four of us had dinner with the "kids". She seemed friendly and kind. I liked her and she told me, "We will always be friends." Later, after Brian's arrest, she declared that she no longer wanted to talk. There are a lot of emotions around domestic violence. My discussion with her may have triggered unpleasant memories she would rather not revisit.

That evening, while sleeping, I must have exhaled deeply in my sleep. This angered Brian to such an extent that at 2:30 a.m., he shouted that I breathed too loud. I softly mentioned I did not have adequate room in our bed, as he was all the way over on my side.

"Shut the fuck up! I will sleep where the fuck I want to!" he screamed so loudly that my ears rang.

I felt like I had been punched in the gut. Being assaulted verbally at 2:00 a.m., just out of deep sleep is confusing, to say the least, and the next morning, he acted like nothing had happened. He even came over to the hospital to have lunch with me.

You should understand that having no frame of reference for behaviors like these, I was often too shocked to respond. Being so far away from friends and family, I felt frightened to make any sort of a move. It was simply too bizarre to comprehend the slow escalation of abuse taking place. Besides, there was still so much I did not know about him.

I consulted a therapist to schedule a meeting after asking Brian to join me to smooth out issues we might need to address. At first, he agreed, but he immediately began to impose conditions and said, "If you are going there to win, forget it. You are better at talking than I am." He changed his mind and then reversed his position.

Brian refused to go, spewing that I was the one who needed to be fixed, not him. My therapist informed me in no uncertain terms that I needed to move out until we could work this out. She said my relationship had all of the classic signs of an abusive one. I was in shock. It was happening to me. Me? Still, I could not bring myself to do it. That day, he left a flower on my car. Subtle gesture, but such is an emotional breadcrumb that we hang onto when we're in the thick of living life with an abuser.

We decided that weekend on an unusually sunny and warm day to take our long stroll through town. Heading down a street we had never walked, I pointed out a lovely porch setting with adorable furniture. "What the fuck do you think? That I can't see it, too?" Brian barked. I was unprepared for his anger and had no idea what had set him off. I turned quietly away and walked home alone. He arrived home two hours later and apologized sincerely, later claiming he did not understand what he had done wrong.

It was impossible to predict what would unleash this bear's anger. Mostly it was not the things I would think, but little moments that had no rhyme or reason. Loving and romantic texts would come each day, but once home, he had little patience for me or my peccadillos.

I noticed his drinking was escalating. Oftentimes, I went to bed early and as I settled in, I could hear him going into the liquor cabinet, bottles and ice cubes clinking as he poured bourbon or vodka. Typically, we would have a glass or two of wine with dinner and then I was done, but in the mornings, I noticed the bottle was often empty or left with nothing more than a sip left in the bottle. I began to watch the levels of liquor in the cabinet, and realized he had been replacing bottles without my knowledge.

Later, we stopped at True Value and I pointed out some attractive patio furniture, excited by the prospect of spring and barbeques on the deck of our new home. He completely ignored me, acting like he did not hear a word I was saying as I pointed out the sets in the brochure. "Brian, look, this would be perfect for the deck." No response.

Later, Brian said, "I thought it would be good training for you," as if he were teaching me that I would only be heard when he deemed it important, my desires and wishes pushed away until such time as felt necessary to address. I felt abandoned and ashamed I was tolerating such treatment, while shocked to hear his assessment of it as "training".

He would have some training of his own very soon.

Brian headed to Seattle to settle business matters with his sister, and I decided to inspect the house to see if I could find anything unusual. What I found were bottles of alcohol, mostly vodka, stashed all over the house; a half empty bottle in his filing cabinet, empty bottles in the garage trash, several bottles stashed in his workbench. He was drinking even more than I knew, in secret. I poured them down the drain, something twelve-step programs advise against.

Doing anything to "help" the alcoholic is discouraged, as interfering in any way will derail the alcoholic from facing his or her own consequences and can cause additional harm; by not allowing the alcoholic to meet his consequences as they happen, one delays the inevitable outcome an alcoholic must meet before they choose or are forced to get help.

Since marijuana had recently become legal in Washington, and we traveled there frequently, Brian bought quite a bit of the edibles and other accoutrements available in stores. Bigwig Sis also loved her edibles. We had extended conversation over dinner about a smorgasbord of highs to experience. I did try a hard candy and didn't like it. She was totally aware of Brian's drug and alcohol abuse, but she condoned and encouraged his use of drugs and alcohol by participating in it and using it with him. Her husband also used and encouraged. Marijuana is not my preference, but to be clear, I did use it once or twice at his suggestion to be amenable and to relieve menstrual cramps.

At dinner, Brian and his brother in-law kept stepping outside to smoke a marijuana vape pen. It was an evening of booze and drugs again.

Although I am sure it was against the law, he flew to Sitka, suitcase loaded with motley weed, and where possession of an ounce of marijuana is legal, suitcases chock full.

CHAPTER 16

Faintly Hearing Wedding Bells

"The human heart has hidden treasures, in secret kept,
in silence sealed; The thoughts, the hopes, the dreams,
the pleasures, whose charms were broken if revealed."
—*Charlotte Bronte*

To CLARIFY, I was still not aware of my fiancée's past substance abuse history in its totality. When we met, he explained he had a past history of cocaine abuse, which he ended in the 1990s, never to be touched again.

He said alcohol had never been a problem and that if I did not like the pot, he did not have to use it and that he would stop. Much later, he denied ever saying that, but he broke so many of his promises that I doubt he could have kept track of all the lies.

I noticed he did not consume alcohol in the presence of either his own mother or his stepmother and each time I asked him, he had a different explanation. "My mother stopped drinking years ago." "My stepmom thought my problem was alcohol, not drugs." "We did not want her to know it was drugs, so we told her it was alcohol."

Amidst a few days where I shot more questions at him, he wrote me the following email:

You are like a magnet. My compass always swings in your direction. When I think of you, I feel pure love. Know that. The happiest day of my life was the day we walked the long beach in Hawaii. I've had good days my love but that was a mind-blowing experience. I have never felt the universe quite so perfectly aligned. I will never give up on us.

Ever,

Brian

The next thirty days were such bliss. He was considerate, loving, sweet, and kind. We enjoyed each other's company, and I called a wedding planner to begin making the arrangements for our Hawaii beach wedding.

One night, while happily under the influence, he told me he wanted to buy my dream wedding gown and pay for the entire affair because he loved me that much. The next morning, when I asked him if he remembered what he said, he said, "No, I do not." I didn't mention the dream gown again. However, that day, I texted my fiancée from work and he responded that there were tears in his eyes; he was thrilled that I had finally begun to plan our wedding.

That evening, after I expressed concern about the wedding without thinking it through, but always expecting a basic level of support and consideration, an argument broke out over dinner that showed me we were in no condition to plan a wedding. Once again, I made the mistake of expressing how I felt and expressing a need. He was so angered that he verbally attacked me, shouting and yelling because of my "unreasonable" expectation that we would be alone on our honeymoon.

The tension was palpable. I called our planner the next day and told her we were going to hold off, realizing we were not ready to be married. I had been an inch from signing a contract for the venue.

Brian emailed me at work, explaining he had been discussing

the venue we had under consideration for our wedding. An acquaintance from Merrill Lynch, who had recently been married there, said it was beautiful. I felt the tension under the surface. Then I saw a text on my phone asking if the wedding was still on.

I underestimated his worries and disregarded wedding planning in favor of finishing up renovations on our new home and the trip we were planning to Maryland in a few weeks, thinking we would reevaluate later.

Several days later, although things had calmed down, another petty argument broke out and he threatened me with coming home from work to find my clothes in our driveway. I replied that he would regret doing something like that to me and threatened him right back. "I will destroy you," I said. "Don't ever do anything like that to me."

"Are you threatening me?" Brian gasped.

"I would never do anything to hurt you, but if you ever do anything like that, you will not like what happens to you. You just threatened me. What response did you expect?"

I had no idea he was planning to throw my clothes out and that he had done this to his ex-wife years earlier, prior to a vicious physical altercation. (Alaska court records document the court proceedings around his assault on her and her orders of protection, both ordered and rescinded.)

Unbeknownst to me, there had been several threats of violence with one carried out and more than one protective order that she would rescind soon after obtaining it. He had six misdemeanors in his history.

Since AA is anonymous, I had no way to know he had been in the program for several years prior to drinking again. He had also been trained and worked as a substance abuse counselor, before he began to use once again. He knew all the right things to say and do to continue to fool me.

CHAPTER 17

Do Not Go Home Alone Tonight

"That is what the intuition is for: it is
the direct messenger of the soul."
—*Clarissa Pinkola Estes*

MAY FADED INTO June without much trouble. Brian was becoming agitated and annoyed with the construction delays that plagued the renovation of our new ocean-view home. Materials took months to arrive on the barge from Seattle. Wait months for the refund, order again. Tile mis-ordered by the store in Juneau and installed. Tear out the tile, re-order and install new tile. With this mundane cycle, he was growing angry and impatient.

In late June, for Father's Day, we decided to take a charter fishing trip. At the same time, I had an issue with a tenant back in New York and was unable to pay for the part of trip I had offered to when we made plans. I explained this a few weeks earlier and he seemed to accept it with understanding.

Brian's son flew in and we headed out early Saturday morning for what would be an excellent day of fishing, blue skies overhead once out of town. We caught eleven fish and had enough salmon and halibut to last for months to come. It was one of the happiest days of my life. Everyone seemed so content, although I did miss my own son, who was back in New York. Brian hid his feelings very well. The cost of the trip, $2,000, was high, but after inheriting half of $5 million, it should not have exactly created anxiety. It led to a horrible outcome the following week. Brian became angry and sullen, even after I pointed out that he was able to create beautiful experiences for his family as a result of his inheritance.

Although Brian spent quite a bit of money for house renovations and the wonderful day of fishing, he never offered to relieve any debt for me, nor did he stop to inquire as to what I might need, if anything. I had a car loan with a very high interest rate, but he never offered to either loan me money or pay it off.

I was not bothered, as he took care of most of the bills and generously gave me cash each time we traveled, to shop for things I needed. Often, I used a significant portion of it to buy gifts for him.

When I offered a couple of times to pay a bill, he stated that "I will let you know when I need money." I chipped in where I could and bought him gifts and groceries for the house. Still, unknown to me, anger and resentment were simmering, like a slow pot of soup on the stove.

We were planning to head back to the East Coast for my niece's wedding. It had been nine months since I had seen my family.

In an agreement before I relocated, Brian said several trips home each year to see my family would be agreeable to him and promised we could make that happen. He did not seem enthused about our upcoming trip since he had no desire to visit Maryland.

Tensions were high in Baltimore as racial tensions mounted the summer of 2015, between police and blacks, who were outraged at a white police officer's killing of a black child, and who had not been charged with a crime. Riots broke out. Coming from a small town, Brian was agitated at the thought of being in the vicinity.

I came home from work Thursday and Brian suggested we go out to dinner. I asked him to re-pot a plant he had given me weeks earlier that I had kept at my office. The plant disappeared. I did not immediately notice. Next, he tried to pick a fight about not wanting to accompany me on a business trip. I did not engage and agreed that he was not required to go.

Looking back, it might have been better if we had "duked it out", then and there, before the alcohol. Days later, I found the flower, planted outside in the flower bed, a completely opposite action to the one I had requested.

After the five o'clock news, we headed out to our local restaurant for a bite. "I am not drinking tonight," Brian mumbled. "I have some work to do at the other house tonight."

We were seated at the bar, as the place was full of summertime out-of-towners. Brian immediately ordered a martini, followed by a second. He had instantly gone against his own intentions. I realized something was out of sorts when he began to engage in an extroverted way with the servers. It was not like him, yet he did not seem angry or otherwise upset. He was leering at one of the young women we knew with an odd look, too. I suddenly felt off kilter. I could not figure out what was going on and when he made an angry comment about "my" upcoming trip, I said in a soothing manner, "It's not my trip, honey. It's our trip." He did not reply. Something was up; I could feel it, a vibrating sensation ever so subtly.

Looking back, I can see the evening was planned in advance. I wonder if, when Brian looks back, he realized his one mistake. It turned out to be a costly one for him. He did not know who I was. Just as in many ways, I did not know the monsters lurking in his mind, he did not know that after a lifetime of backing down, I would not back down anymore.

Men might give significant consideration to messing with fifty-something women. We are fierce and ready to take on the world, knowing we are over the horizon of our lives; but many of us are just beginning to come into our own. We have had experience and risk taking is less appealing. It seems so much more is at stake.

We arrived home and Brian settled onto the couch, making no effort at conversation before leaving to work at the other house. He switched on the new flat screen and turned the channel on a reality show of the genre he knew I would never watch. Again, *bait*. I did not take it and instead, mentioned I was headed upstairs to shower as he read the newspaper. He held it up in front of his face, blocking me out, intentionally rude.

My shower was a long one, as I had to shave my legs. When I came out thirty minutes later, he was still reading the local paper, which is all of four pages on weekdays. Brian said he would come to bed shortly. I settled into our bed with a book and waited for him.

Two hours later, he had not come to bed. It felt unusual, off balance. I stepped down the stairs and quietly asked him, "Honey, why don't you come to bed? We can snuggle for a while before we go to sleep?"

"Fuck you!" he shouted. "I will fucking come to bed!" I recoiled and started back up the stairs to bed as he followed me, berating me for asking him to be close to me.

I attempted to diffuse the situation by getting into bed, but he began calling me a "cunt", with a tone in his voice unlike I had ever heard. I was scared and nervous, not sure where this was going, but a voice in my head urged me to stay calm.

Next, Brian stormed out the front door. Then I heard the car door slam. I peered out of the bedroom window, looking directly down on him in the rain, in our driveway. He was tearing my freshly dry-cleaned clothes out of the plastic and tossing them into the driveway, soaked with rain. His stayed clean and dry. He placed them on the couch when he came inside.

I was in disbelief and ventured outside to collect my clothing, quietly gathering it from the driveway. He approached me and I asked, "Brian what is going on?" He just gave me crooked, sideways glace with hatred pouring out of his beautiful blue eyes.

Brian came inside, all the while calling me a cunt. He settled onto the couch and I realized he was drunk. "You're right, I am drunk," he slurred.

"You are an alcoholic," I declared.

"You are right. I am an alcoholic," he chuckled. Then he proceeded to call me a cunt over and over, emphasizing the "C" like a hard "K", spittle hitting me as he hissed his words. When I asked him to stop, Brian refused.

He threatened me with further malicious actions. I called the police. His behavior was unprecedented and up to this moment, had been verbal slights and brief arguments. I had not witnessed anything remotely like this, and it was horrifying. He laid down on the couch like a child and stayed there until the police came, curled up like a toddler in his fuzzy blue fleece bathrobe, insisting he was doing nothing wrong, intoxicated and slurring in his low, gravelly voice. They warned him to leave me alone and counseled me that I should consider leaving for the night, either to a hotel or the shelter. I was incensed and asked about my rights.

Under Alaska law, regardless of ownership, anyone residing in a property has equal rights to the property if they have resided there for one year.

Since I was not the one causing trouble, I was angered and felt disturbed that I should have to leave. I refused and suggested they arrest him, but at this point, he had not broken any laws. The officers, all male, were supportive, but obviously frustrated that I would not leave for the night.

Brian was contrite with the officers but very drunk. He made no sense, and mumbled, denying any behavior required a phone call to police.

"Officer," he said, "does it look like I am doing anything to her? I'm just right here on the couch." His voice was childlike and passive. The officers knew Brian well and acted with tolerance yet sternly commanded for him to stop harassing me. We agreed that I would go to bed, and he should leave me alone.

There is no law that says you cannot be drunk in your own home. But when other poor souls are in the house, maybe there should be!

The police departed and suggested I call back if he did not settle down.

Within moments, Brian began harassing me again, calling me a cunt, angry with me for calling the police into his home. "I can do anything I want to you. The police are my friends. Obviously, I did nothing wrong, as I was not arrested." I stayed mostly silent but called the police again as he frightened me with his next statement. "I can do anything I want to you. Nobody is going to help you. This is my town. People hate you here. You're SO fucking fabulous. Cunt. Cunt. Cunt." He must have said it one hundred times. Then, "Two fucking blowjobs in a year, two fucking blowjobs are all you could manage. You are ugly and you look old. Your body is disgusting. By the time you are sixty, you will be hideous. Your pussy doesn't even feel good, and it smells bad."

I simply had no ability to respond to such cruelty. I had never once been spoken to like this in almost fifty years. His words were incomprehensible. I had no tools to handle the treatment. The words sunk in. Maybe people did hate me. Brian had few close friends.

Although he served as a volunteer on five boards and worked for twelve years for his employer, no friends called to ask us to dinner, parties or Super Bowl. We received only one invitation to a neighborhood holiday party in one year. Maybe it *was* me, I thought. I was just too different for the people here with my nice clothes, lipstick and makeup. I had lived in Sitka for nine months and had made a few friends, but still, invites were few and far between. People were nice enough to me, but at least one told me Brian was not one of her favorite people. Then on the local flights, I heard one scandalous tale after another about him.

Later, I would find out his lack of friends had nothing whatsoever to do with me. Although Brian served on five boards and was on his church consistory, his good deeds did not help much in controlling his anger. One man, who served with him on a board in the past, informed me that upon Brian's resignation, people cheered. His oppositional tactics and surliness would not be missed.

I had no time to think about this while Brian became more aggressive and threatening by the second. I called the police again. They arrived this time annoyed but professional and told him to leave me alone before they departed. "We know you, Brian, but we will not hesitate to arrest you if you keep this up." Outside, the officer quietly explained to me it would be a book-and-release for disorderly conduct, which might anger him even more.

Brian appeared to be compliant and in agreement with them, but before the officers were out the front door, his verbal assault began again. This time, the police heard him and turned back up the stairs and commanded that if he uttered one more word to me, they would take him in. They also insisted they would sit outside the house to make sure he was behaving. It was after midnight.

Brian remained quiet until 5:00 a.m., at which time he resumed calling me a cunt, over and over and over, pushing the bedroom door open. I got up and showered, preparing to go to work. His vitriol had not lessened even one iota over the past five hours.

At my desk at 7:00 a.m., I tried to be effective. Then the texts started coming in. Full of hatred and anger as he accused and threatened me some more, I did not respond. It did not occur to me that he did not show up to work, or even call in sick. Typically, overly responsible, his not calling into work was not typical behavior. I had never known him to do this even once.

Someone had to intervene.

I called his sister, his daughter and his former priest and close friend, Dave. According to Brian, Dave was the only person on earth who knew all of his history. I doubt he knew everything. Maybe that explains why, according to Brian, when he asked Dave's daughter out for date years earlier, she declined after speaking with her father.

Dave seemed willing to help, unlike the others. He said he would stop by work to see Brian. He tried to call several times, but Brian would not answer phone calls or texts from anyone that day. Before ending the call with me, Dave asked me why I thought his was happening. I explained I knew a great deal of his past history of abuse. I was probably too shaken to explain I knew of his past drug abuse; however, I did not know he was an alcoholic in the truest sense of the word.

Prior to ending the call, Dave said, "Adriana, whatever you do, do not go home alone tonight." But where did he think I would go?

Since I had no idea if Brian had gone to work, and I could not imagine he would not, I went home for lunch. In repose on the couch, disheveled and in his bathrobe, Brian was still obviously intoxicated. I could not imagine where the booze was, since we had nothing left in the liquor cabinet. I noticed he had even drunk the small amount of Sambuca we had left, despite hating the taste of licorice.

Brian immediately began berating me. "You expect me to make nice after you called the police to my home. Fuck you. Go away." He said I brought nothing to the relationship and kept insisting I turn my entire paycheck over to him for bills. Since I paid all of my own bills and earned nothing close to his salary, I tried to reason with him, but there is no reasoning with a drunk and no winning an argument. For a moment, there was a brief pause, I attempted to placate him with agreement, but as I watched him contemplate his actions, he decided to launch back into his verbal assault.

I suddenly assessed that this was becoming a much worse situation than I had realized and took out my phone, turned on *record* and placed it on the coffee table in front of him.

I hoped he would realize what I was doing as he continued to threaten me, telling me to leave his house. "I am not going anywhere, Brian. This is my home." Seething now, I refused to allow him to bully me.

"I know how this works," he said in a sly tone. "I've done this before. *Obviously*, I have not broken any laws. I was not arrested last night. *Obviously*, I've done nothing wrong. What do you bring?" Insults about a property I had in foreclosure came next, followed by his stating he was going to Hawaii alone, not to

Baltimore with me, as scheduled.

"If you want to go, you can pay for it," he said, admitting he did not want to travel to New York and that I should cancel the trip and go to Hawaii with him instead. He paused as I feigned agreement in my pathetic attempt to diffuse his rage. For a moment, he stopped, trying to sort out how to respond, but he was very drunk and unable to reason.

The tape captured, "Go the fuck away. You think you can call the police to my home three times, and then fucking make nice? Fuck you. Fuck you. You have not done anything. You don't pay for shit. Pay your own freight. You are a bitch. You are a cunt. Go away. You are a fucking cunt. Go away. A drama queen. Cunt—Can't Understand Normal Thinking."

The insults went on and on, unabated. I stood up to him as strongly as I could. There is simply no arguing with an alcoholic.

As he gave me the middle finger, Brian continued his verbal insults, threatening me with him selling his house and forcing me out. "This is my house. I don't want to see you here anymore. I've done this before. I know what to do."

After close to ten minutes of recording his verbal insults, I went back to work, realizing it was useless to reason with a drunk. I worked the remainder of the day, feeling safer there and hoping the hours would allow Brian to sober up and calm down. My nerves were jangled. I could not eat a bite; something that only happens to me in times of extreme stress. I had seriously underestimated his fury, but with a degree in criminal justice and years of true crime reading for sport, perhaps I knew too much to be frightened enough to save myself.

It could not happen to me, I thought. *I'm not that woman.* Never stopping to see that I was that woman, and it was happening to me.

It was just too incomprehensible that I would find myself with a character like this. I could not process it logically enough to understand. I felt I was watching this bizarre thing unfold onto somebody else. I would wonder in the future how I was able to stay so calm.

My therapist later referred to this as *disassociation*.

CHAPTER 18

Coffee with Bleach

*"If you are silent about your pain, they'll
kill you and say you enjoyed it."*
—*Zora Neale Hurston*

AT 5:00 P.M., I walked in the front door of our split level, two floors
below Brian at entry. A large black suitcase blocked the door. *Leave,*
it implied. Immediately, I smelled a strong odor. It took a second
to realize it was bleach. *Oh, good,* I thought, *Brian must be doing
laundry.*

Hoping the storm had passed, I assumed he felt bad for his
behavior and maybe he had been cleaning after sobering up. He
would often clean when he felt anxious as a way to blow off steam.
Logic did not apply, but I could not have imagined the events of the
next few minutes if I had been Ann Rule.

First, noticing the quiet and not seeing Brian on the couch, I was
relieved. I made a slice of toast, as I had not eaten a bite all day. I ate
half and felt something was not right. It was eerily quiet.

I headed up the stairs and looked ahead to the master bedroom,
spotting Brian's feet as he was flat on his stomach, naked on the bed.
Out of my peripheral vision, I saw the spare bedroom where my

clothes were kept and saw drawers pulled out and clothing strewn all over the room. It reminded me of a CSI crime scene on TV. I stepped into the room to see my closet, empty of all of my clothes, hangers lopsided, thinking he had stuffed all in the suitcase. Bad enough. I tried to make sense fast, to attempt to put order in my mind.

"Fuck you," Brian growled, realizing I was home.

I scanned the master bedroom and saw a large piece of thin plastic crumpled on the floor. It made no sense, but still, I wondered what he had been up to. Since his own father committed suicide when Brian was a teenager, I wondered if that was what he had been trying to do.

"Brian," I asked, "where are my clothes?" He rolled over, gave me a crooked grin and I saw he was still very intoxicated.

He rose out of the bed, staggering into the hallway and led me to the bathroom where I saw almost every beautiful piece of clothing I owned in a pile in the bathtub and a gallon of empty bleach on the floor. Coffee grinds were sprinkled all over the top of the pile, along with a full pot of hot water to finish whatever the bleach did not destroy. Most of the clothes had been eaten through from the bleach. They were still warm. It was a feeling of horror, but maybe more like disbelief. Seeing it was incomprehensible. I still can't quite believe someone did this.

Clothing to me was a statement, my presentation to the world, art and beauty. I had modeled in my younger years and always the girly girl, had enjoyed looking stylish daily. I had expensive designer clothes and suits from my former career as a realtor. Dresses and gowns purchased for events and family occasions over the years were all destroyed, along with my everyday work wardrobe.

The new $300 bathmats were bleached, and the bathroom counter had been scraped clean of all items and smashed into the sinks; the bathroom was a natural disaster. I felt strangely calm though. Finally, a visual representation of the beast that could not be denied or rationed away like verbal assaults.

I looked at him, shaking my head and said, "Really, Brian? I just wanted to come home and wave the white flag, and maybe have dinner." Cell phone in hand, I dialed the police. They arrived in what seemed like seconds.

Although I did not hear it, I would learn he admitted to the police that he had done the crime in retaliation for my having called the police the night before. The officers took photos of the scene and asked me to sort through all of the clothes, itemizing each piece and giving an approximate value for each item.

Brian was separated from me as one of the officers took me to the kitchen and explained Brian would be arrested. Although I have read the police records and agree with them, I have no memory of anything I said to them that evening. In his report, the officer said he had advised me to leave and kept asking questions I do not remember. Later, the police officer would say I kept repeating words he could not hear, in a low voice, words not making sense and confused.

Police are often injured in response to calls for domestic violence. It is one of the riskiest situations for police to handle and tempers can swing erratically and quickly. In my case, I think the police did a respectable job in handling the situation. They did not minimize me or make me feel at fault for the crime at all. Although one officer did suggest that I go to a hotel Thursday evening, I refused and stood my ground. I was intent on seeing the situation through to whatever end it was destined for, never thinking I might be risking life or limb.

Eying the clothes, the officer asked me how much value my clothing had. I said, "At least $5,000, officer." He then explained the crime was a felony due to the dollar amount of damage. Brian would spend the night in jail and be arraigned the following afternoon.

"Make a list of each item and its value," he sighed, scanning the display of madness. I was thinking about the fumes and handling the clothing with so much bleach on them. I opened all of the windows I could.

I listed each item on a yellow legal pad and put its retail price next to it.

I tried to save a few pieces and washed them in the machines at home, but weeks later, realized the bleach had destroyed them with small areas of color gone, making them unusable. Looking back, I should have listed those, too, but I thought I had saved them at the time. Doing laundry for hours that night, I understand this act was as a result of shock. I was just on automatic.

At times, the fumes overtook me. I had to lie down on the bedroom floor and breathe before I could go back to sorting. I put everything in garbage bags and prepared to deliver them to the police station as evidence. Later, after having delivered them, I grasped that my clothes were on inside-out. The shock kept me moving, but I was not really cognizant.

Embarrassed and disheveled from the events of the evening, I sat down for a cup of tea with my friend, Mary, who came to support me, bearing food and items to comfort me. She did her best to persuade me to vacate and run. I refused, and this would be my stance going forward. I would have possession of the house for seven months.

I was able to sleep a little that night after sorting clothes and having been given comfort from Mary, who insisted I leave because she believed he was going to kill me. I decided to stay, knowing at least for that night I was safe from his abuse and harassment. He was rotting in jail.

It was a fitful sleep, and I had no idea what would come next.

Later the next morning, the police called and gave me the opportunity to attend the arraignment at 1:00 p.m., telephonically. I did just that and explained to the magistrate that Brian had a substance abuse problem and needed treatment. Others from Sitka, who had legal matters to attend to, were on the call and overheard the entire scenario.

In interviews with other women who have been in relationships where domestic violence was a component, I realized we all have such different thoughts and reactions. Several told me they never called police. "I was raised not to make waves," one said. "It never occurred to me to call the police." This comment was made after one woman who asked that her name not be revealed, confessed that after her husband had beaten and raped her, she never even thought to call police.

Brian was released on $1,000 bail and instructed by the magistrate not to come home, and to stay away from me and my place of employment. He was not to consume alcohol or be in a bar or liquor store. The magistrate only allowed him to come to the house once to gather personal items.

I stayed home and sat quietly while Brian took everything but the kitchen sink, away in his car. At the end, he quietly asked if he could water the flowers. I declined, he was gone, and I was left to a deafening silence and the rest of the weekend. The days would stretch into months as the case cycled through the court system. It was an energy suck of the worst kind. Fatigue alternated with insomnia, fear and anger.

During this time, I would discover he met and had oral sex with a woman he had been stringing along for months, toying with her emotions, one month after I had accepted his proposal of marriage and was to arrive in Seattle, where she lived. Let me not forget to add that there would be several discoveries of this sort as time went on.

After the attack, I sent this email to women in Brian's contact list:

I am writing this in hopes all of you know how fortunate you were to escape the emotional and verbal assaults I have endured this past year as the fiancée of Brian. I know that we all shared contact and maybe sexual relationships with him. This past weekend, Brian was arrested on a felony domestic violence charge after he verbally abused me for over two days during an alcoholic binge that led to rage.

If any of you require substantiation, simply look at the public and free Alaska court records.

I know Brian wrote several of you even after we were engaged and did not disclose that he had committed to me, even though I had relocated to Sitka and was living with him. He was writing to a few of you from his dying mother's bedside while I was rubbing her feet.

During the time, I thought we were in an exclusive relationship, he was seeing others and lied to all of us about his feelings and intentions.

Although Brian later told me he had been guilty of manipulating several women at once, I would be shocked to learn this had never really stopped. It appears that in his deep insecurity, he simply could not help himself from his addiction to the attention of multiple women at once.

This past year has been a year of lies, anger, and manipulation, as I watched his alcoholism progress to a destructive rage that led me to contact his ex-wife and the women's' shelter here in Alaska. He has a prior conviction of DV ten years ago, two DUI's in the 1980s and another DV charge from his ex-wife in the 1990s.

Several restraining orders were issued and withdrawn.

This particular weekend after two days of threats of violence, and in a drunken rage he placed my entire wardrobe in the bathtub and poured bleach and a pot of coffee on my clothing while I was at work. He smashed all of the glass items in the bathroom, tore all leftover clothing out of the dresser and threw it around the bedroom. The police were at my home three times Thursday and once Friday when they finally arrested him.

Brian was arrested and released on bail Saturday. He was facing up to five years in jail, ten years' probation and a $50,000 fine, for doing over $10,000 in damage to my property. I am sharing this to prevent you from falling for his lines if he reaches out to you.

This is an email I received back:

Wow. I am blown away by your email. I did see Brian in early May of last year when he was in Seattle taking his mom to Virginia Mason. We had been talking on and off for months. No, I did not know anything about you. We made plans to be together the next month when he was in Seattle for his nephew's (or niece's) graduation. I even bought expensive tickets to The Triple Door for dinner and music as a surprise for us. I told him before he left. Then nothing. I texted, emailed.... nothing. I finally wrote and told him to use the tickets on whoever he was obviously involved with when he came to back to Seattle. I never heard anything more from him after that. I was really hurt and finally looked at his Facebook page. Clicked on your profile and saw your status was "Engaged to Brian". Since before he was with me. I wrote him an email telling him what a prick he was and that I wondered if his fiancée was aware of his cheating. Of course, I never heard back. I am curious as to how you found me. I hope you will be okay. I guess I dodged the bullet that you didn't.

Later, I asked her if their relationship was sexual. "Yes," she replied. "Oral sex."

I was in possession of his iPad, which had been misplaced during the commotion. It turned up and I saw his recent texts and emails. His daughter had been telling folks in town I had smashed it with a hammer in order to offer a reason for his committing the crime. I weighed my option on whether or not to disclose I had the iPad. After texting with Brian's ex-wife, I sent her photo of the IPad in one piece, to prove I had not provoked the attack. She admitted Allison had also told her this story. Unfortunately, once learned I was in possession of it, he wasted little time and wiped the iPad clean remotely. I no longer had access to his emails.

Brian's ex, so friendly to me before, was now becoming angry that I was pursuing this, something she had not chosen to do despite having endured several physical assaults by Brian. Victims exist solely as a projection of others. What they say about the victim says more about them than anything else.

His daughter, involved in an enmeshed relationship with her father, was a victim, too. She had been the witness to his beating of her mother and vacillated between supporting him and protecting him. Growing up in an emotionally unstable home, especially as the oldest child, was familiar to me.

Brian had relayed stories of Allison's outbursts as a child, stating, "We filled a tub with ice cold water and put her in it." I only felt empathy toward her suffering and victimization, as yet another and maybe most injured person Brian had damaged. According to Brian, she experienced such extreme fits of temper, the ice-cold water was the only way he could "shock" her out of it.

On more than one occasion, I had gone to her in fear. Each time she was kind and understood how frightening his behavior could be, telling me "you can't stay with someone who treats you like this." In the end, her own issues would surface as she defended him without hesitation, a loyal daughter blinded by his abuse, and a victim, raised by an abuser.

Allison came by the house after Brian's release from jail for a few personal items. "You're leaving Sitka, right?" she asked. "It's a small town. It will be hard for you to stay here."

"Allison," I responded, "I am in such a state of shock, I am not making any decisions right now. I did nothing wrong though, and I don't plan on leaving. I have a good job and friends here. I have a right to stay in my home for up to a year."

Her expression twisted into a mix of horror and disbelief. She knew exactly what it would mean to her family to have me stay in town. She was not pleased. I can only imagine her embarrassment from having a dad like him. I had one and knew the inescapable experience only too well.

The most important thing I did was to read all of Brian's past emails and texts. I saw many emails he had sent to other women, and immediately notified all of them of his violence, telling them he would be reaching out. I knew he could not stand to be alone. One of these women would surely be a target.

Most were supportive and expressed great empathy, but one, a past lover from Anchorage, was reaching out via text to help him wipe the iPad clean and was supportive of his plight. She was a recovering alcoholic with arrests and a checkered past of her own, which I discovered after checking the public Alaska criminal records database, where anyone can go and check to see if someone has a criminal record, free of charge.

Her email response to me though was telling.

Good God! I am sorry you had to experience the horror of abuse! I saw his alcoholism progressing. I feel fortunate to have escaped this tragedy. I wish you well..."

Brian had confessed to making serious mistakes with regard to women in his recent past, but mostly blamed them for the breakups, after some discovered he was sleeping with more than one at a time, lying to each. He also traveled frequently to meet women, often sleeping with up to three in the same day, according to stories he relayed to me. Since his divorce about eight years earlier, his dating life had been a revolving door of woman after woman.

Restless and full of anxiety, I walked, cooked and watched movies in order to calm myself. Sunday evening, the district attorney called my home. We reviewed the crime and whether or not to pursue a felony charge in the case. The DA was pragmatic and even tempered but stated the police officer had mentioned this was as deliberate as any crime he had seen in quite some time and was disturbing to see, even for him. She was compassionate, with just the right amount of concern.

The DA and her assistant and victim advocate sat with me in

the courtroom. They coached me through every aspect of the prosecuting, never making false promises or guarantees of conviction. In fact, one day when I asked for her opinion and stating my own that "Brian's lawyer will not take this case to trial, he knows he has a loser", she looked me square in the face and stated crisply, "I do not take any case for granted. Look at OJ."

I visited the DA several times throughout my case, sharing items of clothing Brian had damaged, such as a pair of panties he had poured bleach on, damaged only in the crotch area, bras destroyed by the bleach. Such intimate things damaged had threatening implications. She was always level-headed and thanked me for sharing my point of view with her. Later, I used this same pair of panties as evidence to the judge of Brian's direct and personal attack on me.

Never are women's chances of being murdered higher than during a separation from her intimate partner. Evan Stark, in his book, *Coercive Control*, explains the statistics and conditions under which this can happen. I did not know it then, but my fears were well-grounded. In my experience, the more visible and vocal the victim is, with respect of course, the more consideration the case receives. I did not take up time unnecessarily, but I did let them know I was present when it was important, always presenting myself as rational and capable and reasonable, always firmly insisting on prosecution and consequences for Brian, that were to the fullest extent allowed by law.

The court granted a short-term restraining order and later, obtained an order that prevented Brian from contacting me for one year. While a few in town felt sorry for Brian and believed he needed help, not jail, they could not have been more mistaken. In my estimation, what had happened to me might never have occurred if women he had harmed before me had held him accountable. He had at least six prior misdemeanors and other slaps on the wrist, but nothing commensurate with his crimes that would alert me or anyone else of the behavioral issues he had.

Next, the grand jury convened and subpoenaed me to testify. I was surprised at my vulnerability, shaking as I gave testimony on the events and the items damaged. Seeing photo after photo of the damaged clothing disturbed me. I cried in front of a room of total strangers, who, judging by the expressions on many of their faces, were shocked at the crime. They chose to issue an indictment with ten minutes of hearing my testimony, preceded by that of the police officer. Brian was fired, after twelve years of employment, from his state job a few days after his arrest, losing both his salary and benefits of close to $80,000.

In the midst of the case, I worked part-time on weekends in the art gallery to help defray the cost of my therapy and to stay busy.

Allison strolled in unannounced one day flipping her long strawberry blonde hair, informing me that as a courtesy, she was stopping by to tell me she would be going into the house I lived in to gather some things.

"Jim [the lawyer] said I don't even have to tell you," she said, flipping her hair once again. "I am just trying to be respectful." I am sure that Jim would not have advised illegal action, and after she left the store, I remembered I had changed the locks. Still at work, however, I was agreeable enough and we decided to meet there after work.

After speaking with the police and getting confirmation that entry by her was illegal, I told Allison I would be happy to give her what she wanted from the house, but that I was not comfortable with anyone going there now. She seemed miffed and once she discerned that I had called the police for advice, she said it was probably a "misunderstanding", backing off without further discussion. I am not sure she has ever been told "no" about anything she wanted to do.

Later, I placed her items in a plastic bag and left them outside the house for her to have, reminding her that I would give her any of her belongings she wanted out of the house. Although it had not been her residence for over a year, she still felt she should be allowed to enter as she pleased, continuing to assert her right to "stop by" later that evening. I simply replied that my plans that evening would prevent me from being there to see her.

The DA informed me that if found guilty, Brian would have to pay restitution for the damaged property and any medical bills associated with the crime. She also said it would take six months to resolve the case. I shuddered but accepted her estimate with some resignation. She asserted that she would prosecute the case whether or not I was involved.

CHAPTER 19

Secrets of the Alaska Criminal Records Database

*"Information about the package is as
important as the package itself."*
—*Frederick W. Smith*

I BEGAN SEEING a therapist and sought support and council from
Sitkans Against Family Violence (SAFV), the shelter in Sitka. My
therapist, having known Brian for over twenty years, had worked
with him years earlier in the fish processing plants in Sitka. She
offered insights into his history and character I could never have
known otherwise. That therapist didn't want to show me the photo
of his wife's face because "the same thing could have happened to
me". She was wonderful. In a small town, everyone knows each
other. Brian was generally known in and around Southeast Alaska
as a womanizer, a violent, angry drug user with an alcohol problem,
who abused women. It must be tough to hold his head up around
town. Maybe he disassociates to survive.

The executive director of SAFV, an Italian woman originally
from the East Coast like me, was the best person I could have met.
A longtime Sitka resident, she knew Brian and explained that the
beating had given his ex-wife was one of the worst she had ever seen,

and that the photo of her badly damaged face had been kept on file for years. She also informed me that several women had needed the SAFV shelter when, after being guests in his home, had fled in fear of his rage, leaving town on the first plane out of town. I soon met one of them myself and she knew of at least one other. These women educated me about my perp and domestic violence in general. She and the other women who work there permitted me to sit and rant out my hysterical disbelief at the situation I found myself in. They offered me a room at the shelter and gave me kindness I could not have imagined, accompanying me to every court hearing, calling me every evening to check in on me, and explaining how the proceedings would unfold. More than any other form of support, the advocates at SAFV gave me the strength to move forward with courage and conviction. This is not one of those events in life to experience alone. I required a great deal of support, and I accepted all that was offered.

I contacted the reverend at Brian's Episcopal Church and explained the ordeal. I had seen an email he sent her shortly after the attack, explaining he was having a hard time understanding, while knowing he was wrong, how after damaging a "few pieces" of his fiancée's clothes, he could possibly be facing such extreme consequences. "I will not support him. I will be supporting you," she said." To this day, I admire and respect her for giving me the opportunity to speak with her.

A good friend, Joe Ryan, professor and chair of the Criminal Justice Department at Pace University in Manhattan, told me that batterers *always* minimize their crimes, referring to them as "mistakes". This is a common tendency of sociopaths as well; they are unable to take responsibility for their actions.

Intimate Partner Abuse Education Programs have had dismal results, according to Ryan, as the criminals never quite admit to themselves the damage they have done to others, so they will continue to repeat the pattern that author Evan Stark deems in his book,

Coercive Control. Coercive control is a "strategic pattern of behavior designed to exploit, control, create dependency and dominate. The victim's everyday existence is micro-managed and her space for action as well as potential as a human being is limited and controlled by the abuser".

Stark both supports Ryan's point and goes further in illustrating that the tactics, complexities and effects of psychological abuse create an unequal power dynamic (whether financial, mental, physical, or all), making it difficult to leave the abusive situation. Many psychologists consider coercive control a form of brainwashing—the victim's identity is essentially stripped over time, and is replaced by narrative (views, needs and desires) that the abuser creates and implants.

When I think about the insults that were hurled at me hundreds of times, I must admit that they sunk into my conditioning for a long time. I played that mental tape and didn't refuse the messages until I revamped my life, inside-out.

Sitka, similar to the rest of the state of Alaska, has a high rate of domestic violence and violent crimes. Close to half of the women who live there have been involved in a crime of domestic violence to include assault and rape and possibly murder. Rarely does violence involve a woman as the perp, as in the case of Jane Reth, who, in the mid-1980s, shot her husband and chopped him up with an ax, depositing his body parts in undisclosed trash cans around Sitka, never to be found. Many years later, she was apprehended after confessing to her second husband and sentenced to thirty-six years in prison by the same judge, who sat on my criminal proceeding against Brian, showing her little mercy.

On May 6, 1996, 17-year-old Jessica Baggen was walking home from her sister's house after celebrating a birthday. She took the Totem Park trail and was viciously beaten, raped and murdered, grass, dirt and leaves stuffed deep in her mouth and throat until she suffocated. Her case was unsolved until 2020.

In 2012, Lael Grant went missing and has never been found.

Although she had a history of substance abuse, her parked car was found just out of town. She has never been seen again. She was recently declared dead by the courts to give her family closure.

While Sitka has a lower crime rate than the state overall, domestic violence and violence against women is much higher than average and nationwide.

Alaska has the highest murder rate of female victims killed by a male perpetrator in the nation, with 59% of Alaska women reporting intimate partner or sexual violence in their lifetimes. National Coalition Against Domestic Violence reports that 72% of all murder suicides involved an intimate partner and 94% of the victims of these crimes are female.

In interviews with local victims, I have heard some disturbing facts about why others are reluctant to call police when they have been assaulted. For example, "I realized that since I am the sole support, I would have to pay all the court fine and fees." Another said that she would have her abuser released because she had to work and did not have daycare. Since she was the breadwinner, with him in jail and not earning money, there would be no child support.

Domestic violence is a complex issue and leaving is not always a *choice*. Most victims never receive court-ordered restitution and there is not much of a mechanism in place to collect it. Women who have children with their abusers are a topic that requires special attention. They are often bound to the abuser unwillingly and rendered powerless by many complicating factors, which I do not address in my personal story.

Alaska court records are free and accessible to the public. One can simply enter a name and any criminal history associated with the person is available. Brian is listed, and all records support my statements. Older records may be archived but are still available if one visits the city court and requests them. Court professionals use yet another system, which had helped to flag that Brian had six misdemeanors; however, I was not allowed to view those records. Why I was not allowed to view the entire history is beyond me.

In the days following the news printed in our local paper about Brian's arrest and later indictment, people began to approach me. My office in human resources was on the top floor of the hospital. People I had never met walked in and expressed their concerns, shook my hand, sat down across from my desk and explained what they knew. Many had been holding their breath, aware of his past and the abuse his ex-wife had endured. One co-worker confessed she had seen him slap her across the face one day while a few couples were out on a boat for a social outing. Another told me of his ex-wife appearing at work with black eyes and sunglasses.

At the grocery store, people spontaneously opened their arms and hugged me. Many expressed they knew it would come to this, but hoped, after seeing me with him, that Brian had changed. Stories of his taking advantage of those weaker or of less privilege were common, and Brian was reputed to have abused his power at the state housing apartment complexes he managed.

One friend I met a month after Brian was arrested before knowing me told me that seeing us out on walks provoked his sympathy for me thinking, *that's too bad*, with a deep sigh when he saw us together. He had been in high school with Brian and knew of his violent temper. Another relayed a story from Brian as told to him when he was a substance abuse counselor. He told his group he had masturbated all over town! The man who filled me in on this said he was never able to get past the bizarre nature of the tale and wondered why Brian had told this to the group. Perhaps even worse, as a "counselor", Brian was intolerant and lacked compassion for those who had just gained their sobriety.

My prime husband material had been reduced to trash.

CHAPTER 20

For the Love of Boundaries

"Daring to set boundaries is about having the courage to love ourselves, even when we risk disappointing others."
—*Brené Brown*

EACH DAY, I struggled to get up and go to work. During the day, I was irritable and forgetful. At the end of the day, I was exhausted, falling into bed immediately upon return home in those first weeks, wanting nothing but the sweet escape of sleep. Often, I would wake from the smallest of noises, terrified he was going to come back and take the attack even further. I had no idea these were symptoms of post-traumatic stress disorder (PTSD), which I would be diagnosed with soon.

My son flew in for a few days from New York, but I was so traumatized, the visit was not so good. I was relieved when he left, as it was impossible to be strong and act like the mother he knew, "fierce" by his words, and in charge.

I had been brought to my emotional knees and walked through each day in fear, anger and uncertainty, frozen and incapable of making choices, decisions or plans. During this period of time and up until I later vacated our residence, I simply had no idea of what would happen, or if Brian would revisit his violence toward me. I was hypervigilant and my nervous system jarred by small sounds and events I might interpret as intentional, when possibly, they were not.

Dreams were disturbing, with blood and violence. At least once I woke, thinking he was in the bedroom with me. Those dreams were upsetting for days afterward.

Two weeks later, my best friend, Helen arrived. I am sure I was insufferable to be around, irritable and short of temper. I still did not know I had PTSD and that the symptoms were quite normal given the fear and trauma I had experienced. Still, she coped well and stayed by my side for two weeks, cooking meals, cleaning my house and tolerating my rudeness and lack of diplomacy.

One day, we decided to walk a trail I had frequently walked with Brian. We were in the rain for about twenty minutes, on a section of the island well-known for having no phone signal. It was a lovely nature sanctuary, surrounded by trees and tidal marshes. We were walking the boardwalk, when I saw a pair of lower legs from under the tree limbs coming toward us. Brian.

I panicked, but determined not to let him see my fear, I kept walking toward him. He was approaching us head-on. Helen lowered her head, appearing submissive to his approach. I insistently pushed forward, as did he, until I stood in the center of the walk, forcing him off to a T in the side of the walk. "You are breaking the law," I said firmly to him, looking him dead in the eye as he stopped, stepping off to the side of the walk, arms crossed, while staring me icily in the eye as he allowed us to pass.

Shaking and not sure he had not followed us, we left the area and after calling the DA, reported the incident to the police.

We had to build a case, and the police advised me to change the locks and install security cameras around the house to address my concerns about his coming there.

I felt under siege.

Small happenings had monumental impact. I believed Brian was coming to the house after I was in bed. I had seen cigarette butts on the porch. One night, after showering, my toothpaste went missing. I believed he had been in the house. I have no proof he was responsible, yet I could not imagine who else would have done these things.

Later, I discerned whose cigarettes they were (not his), but in active PTSD, the mind convinces one otherwise.

My family and friends wanted me out of Sitka and his house, but I felt strongly about holding his feet to the fire, making his crime visible and ensuring he received every possible consequence for his actions. I felt I had to stay at least until the case was adjudicated. With six misdemeanors on his record, this is a man who apparently got off easily for his errs.

One fact I'd bet most women are not aware of is that officers are required to make an arrest in domestic violence cases. A landmark case in the state of Connecticut is the reason for this: Tracy Thurman was stabbed and nearly killed by her husband after police had visited the home close to twenty times for domestic violence, assaults and threats, displaying a cavalier attitude and at times, not arriving for hours after she had called for help. After her husband attacked her and she sued the state, winning $2.3 million, laws throughout the United States were changed, making arrest mandatory in domestic violence cases, even if the victim does not wish to press charges, according to my friend, Joe Ryan, a former detective with the NYPD.

All of the other women who had been exposed to Brian's violence understandably left town as quickly possible. I refused to back down. Every injustice I ever suffered was going to be released in this circumstance. I believed then as I do now that the abuser should be outed publicly once convicted. Most efforts by criminal justice experts to stem domestic violence have failed, according to Ryan. I discussed the recent case of Brock Turner, the convicted rapist with Ryan and the magnificent "outing" of him in both mainstream and social media.

I also employed that tactic in my case. It is my belief that due to the consequences he received, Brian will think twice before acting out to this extent ever again. Fair or not, Brian was going to bear the brunt of his actions and walk, his head hung in shame around Sitka for some time to come.

One woman, now a resident of Sitka who dated Brian years earlier, and who fled his home for the airport after an outburst of temper, was at my side supporting me the whole way and even sat with me the day of his sentencing. A trial date was set. He went out of state for substance abuse treatment, my damages still unresolved. In Alaska, doing twenty-eight days in treatment counted day for day for jail time, so he avoided jail as a consequence.

I paid another visit to the DA to voice my concern at his departing for treatment while I awaited restitution. "What was so important about him needing treatment now?" I asked. "He has been in rehab at least three times. What is the urgency of his departure and before I am compensated for the damages?"

After rehab, he obtained permission for a trip to Hawaii. While on the island, he sent this Facebook Message to my mother.

Nov 5, 2015

Karen, do you know or have any idea what your daughter is up to in Sitka? She has made it her main job to destroy me. She has seen me lose my job, my status in the community and most of all, my self-respect. She continues to live in my house while I pay all the bills. Her response to me trying to get my house back is PTSD in regard to our falling out. She entertains multiple men in my home, while making sure I know about it. Worst of all, I am not able to fall out of love with her. I just wanted you to know what's going on.

My fear and anger, coupled with no communication from Brian, left me reeling and confused. My instructions to the magistrate had been that he could contact me through his attorney. He never did. Seeing him reach out to my mother, whom he had met just one time, was infuriating, yet I wanted so much to believe he still loved me. I hated him and wanted him back all at once. I was so close to getting on a flight to Hawaii; I am still not sure how or why I did not do it. A small voice in my mind told me I would be in danger. I listened to it.

At this time, I was still waiting for compensation for my damaged clothing and reimbursement for my therapy, not covered by my health insurance. Although I had occupancy of his house and did not have to pay for it, making ends meet in Sitka on a $57,000 salary was not easy. I had lost most of my clothing and the cost of living is staggering. I had no idea how long I would be able to live in his house or how I would move out, since everything I owned was in a storage unit in New

York. Although Alaska law says that regardless of ownership, all residents of the property are afforded equal property rights, the law afforded me little protection with the judge.

Judges in Alaska are known to be liberal, and minimal consequences are imposed on domestic violence offenders. Felony convictions are even rarer. In fact, in talks with my therapist, she mentioned I could not stake my well-being on a conviction. I reeled in shock. The thought that Brian might not be convicted had never occurred to me. I am grateful she thought to prep me for an outcome I never expected. This is how rare felony convictions are in domestic violence cases.

Brian's daughter began texting me in mid-September. This time I realized she was taking pleasure in harassing me as she requested a few items from the house—mainly, her great-grandmother's engagement ring, which her father had given to me.

Looking back, I can see that having failed in her attempt to gain entry to the house earlier that summer, she was again interjecting in an effort to bully me.

Only her fucked up father had the "right" to ask for that ring back.

"I only ask because it is a family heirloom being passed down through generations and that means something to me," Allison wrote. "If it were just a ring my father bought, I would have no reason to ask. I look forward to your answer next week."

This is when I grasped that I was being harassed. Why Allison ever thought she had authority to speak for her father and his intentions is unknown to me. Maybe he asked her to ask me for it, or to inform me of his intentions. I will never know. I cracked and sold the ring in anger for $500.

In the text exchange, I felt threatened and manipulated. Later, I sent an email to close the door on any further conversation, as there was too much coming at me and with PTSD, I was unable to respond properly to even small emotional exchanges. Adrenaline flares blurring logical thoughts. I panicked each time we had contact. I had no idea if she was initiating of her own free will or acting as directed by Brian.

The boundary violations are clear. Requesting a gift be returned was not her right. Besides, I had sold both my rings after the arrest out of fear of not having the money to survive and in anger at his criminal abuse of me and my property.

Although Brian had given me a larger Tiffany diamond that we found in his mother's safety deposit box, he had not asked for the first one back. If I still had the ring today, I would not give it back on principle.

Finding boundaries and taking care of myself instead of others has never been comfortable for me. Taking a stand for my needs was essential to my recovery, and according to my therapist, anyone not 100% supportive of me was not allowed to be anywhere near me at this point in the process.

I highly recommend considering advice like this. Support is essential to recovery.

CHAPTER 21

The Interrogations

*"The only interesting answers are those
that destroy the questions."*

—*Susan Sontag*

NEXT, BRIAN'S LAWYER served me with an eviction order, and I had
to attend a court hearing to determine when I would vacate the residence. The judge, sympathetic but not overly generous, gave me an
additional three months to secure housing, as Sitka rentals were not
easy to find. I would have occupancy until January 31st.

When making his decisions, the lawyer added that there were no
children, insinuating that I alone was not worthy of having the time
to heal in place as I had requested. Instead, he minimized my request
by distorting my condition.

Although this particular lawyer had a great deal of experience
with victims of DV, he was fighting for his client and stated that I
should move out for my own good. "You don't stay in Fallujah after
the war."

"It's not the place; it is the person who did it," I replied.

Brian's lawyer questioned me or made comments that he was not
entirely prepared to handle the answers on. I caught him off guard

several times with my quick responses that undermined his client's position. It was mildly enjoyable to best his attorney once or twice when given the opportunity.

He questioned me at length. I held my ground for the most part, but one cannot be prepared enough to take on a professional attorney. After my hearing, the DA and victim advocate said I did well, as they were listening on the overhead.

I did not always know exactly what to do in the multiple hearings I was required to attend. Looking back, I would have liked to assert myself more with respect to the judge, asking him to consider the law, and give me equal rights to the property and for one year as the law stated. I could also have looked up history in cases like mine to see how long people in my situation had been given. My contacts at SAFV had predicted I would not get one year—and they were right. Asking more questions could have helped me. I did not feel up to it.

I spent several days on the couch emotionally exhausted after this hearing.

CHAPTER 22

Living for Twisted Victories

"The harder the struggle, the more glorious the triumph.
Self-realization demands very great struggle."
—*Swami Sivananda*

PRIOR TO THE trial, Brian's attorney entered a guilty plea to the felony charge.

It was agreed that he would pay restitution of close to $11,000, have no contact with me for one year and that he would be on probation for two years. While on probation, he was not allowed to consume alcohol, or any drug not prescribed by his physician. He was subjected to search of his home, car and person anytime for drug paraphernalia or weapons.

Last, for a man who loved to travel, he had to obtain permission from his probation officer prior to leaving town. Surely, this cramped his style.

Prior to the sentencing, I wrote a post on the Facebook page, Sitka Chatters.

This group, for residents of Sitka, allowed for conversation about topics related to town, the people who live there or just about anything.

I asked for support at the sentencing and also thanked people for offering me support. I was bashed by friends of the family on a few occasions, but most comments were wonderful. A couple of people, for reasons unknown to me, felt I was wrong to assert myself. One young woman, a friend of Allison's and whose own mom had been a victim of violence, claimed I was hurting people I did not know. To this day, I wonder what she meant. I was shocked at the number of personal messages I received from women who had been affected by domestic violence themselves. I knew several of them, and they asked that I keep them anonymous.

In making my case public, instead of keeping it in the shroud of shame and secrecy many victims choose to do, I made sure others in town would not suffer at the hand of my perp. I also felt that the more people who knew, the safer I would be. My choice was my own and I did not expect all victims to do the same thing. Each woman must act according to her own needs and to ensure her own safety.

Many women are afraid they will be murdered, and their children left motherless, which leaves them unable to take an assertive stance such as mine.

I did not have children with my abuser and my own child lived far way in New York. I was willing to risk my own safety but might not have risked that of a younger child. Because I was so open, several people approached me to share their stories and knowledge of other women affected by my perp. Although in most cases, I was unable to get verification and do not mention them, a few prominent and mature women offered me their house keys in case I felt the need to run or hide. Half the court knew this man as one who lived to be a womanizer and scam people. Again, on his way home from asking me to marry him, he stopped to get a blow job! He had no feelings. He mimicked feelings and experiences masterfully. Every sane, sensible person saw this.

Still, at Brian's sentencing almost two months later, his entire family, including Bigwig Sis, flew in for the event and filed into court on December 11, 2015. The only family member not present was his biological sister. She would not have added to the picture-perfect family he was trying to present to the court and would only have embarrassed them all.

Despite having submitted his own psychological evaluation report by a well-credentialed professional, Brian was ordered to submit one to an integrated behavioral and psychological assessment from a local professional and subject to further treatment if recommended by the psychologist.

The judge, to his credit, dressed Brian down, aware that his family was probably not privy to the extent of his crime, noticing their apparent intent to intimidate me by coming, all-together, for the first time to the court.

"It takes a lot more to restore a victim than writing a check. All victims are affected differently, and it seems Ms. Jaymes was greatly affected by this crime. As such, we are going to run your life for the next two years. If we ask you to pee in a cup, you will have to pee in a cup, right then, not two hours later. Ms. Jaymes did nothing to deserve this. We have to make sure nothing like this happens again."

In this hearing, Brian was diagnosed as "alcohol dependent", based on a doctor's report according to the judge.

The judge also noted that due to his age, he presented a rather unique dilemma to the court. He was not a teenager, who the court would have viewed as likely to re-offend yet, given his history, the judge did not think it was unlikely he would not re-offend as a mature adult. He had to take a unique approach to the situation and told Brian in no uncertain terms, "We have to make sure this does not happen again." The judge also took note of Brian's volunteer service. He must have truly been an enigma to the court, who usually sees bad characters that don't function so well in society. This is another sociopathic tendency. Often, they function well in society since they deceive and outsmart unsuspecting people who cross their paths. In an effort to "fit in", they learn how to appear normal.

Brian's lifelong criminal lawyer, who represented him whenever needed, spoke eloquently about Brian's service to his community and his church, citing his volunteer work, yet excusing him because of his alcohol abuse, employing his silver tongue like two opposing swords, to agree that Brian not only knew he had destroyed a good relationship and that I had done nothing to deserve his cruelty, but wanted to publicly apologize to me in court.

I walked out of the courtroom not wanting him to address me directly, coming back only when I knew the judge would not allow it. He instructed Brian to make any statements only to him. In a statement that went something like this, the attorney said, "Judge, I have known Brian for many years, our kids played ball together, and we coached together."

"You mean Mr. —," the judge corrected. "Brian has a problem with alcohol. As long as he does not drink, he can keep the genie in the bottle, but if he drinks, the genie comes out," Harry said.

Herein lies the fallacy of domestic violence and substance abuse. Lawyers and judges blame the alcohol or substance involved. The truth is that while there may be a link between substance abuse and violence, the substance is not the cause. It is the vehicle. It gives permission for the abuser and provides the ammunition abusers need to carry out their plan. It is not, however, the root cause. Most often, when Brian was verbally abusive, he had not been drinking.

Victims have an opportunity to speak. I submitted a four-page victim impact statement for the judge to read. He asked me if I had anything to say and I asked him if I he had read the statement. He acknowledged that he did, and I had no need to read it aloud. It was obvious he had read it, as many of his comments reflected my statements and requests, while he sentenced Brian. Scheduled to last only twenty minutes, the sentencing lasted an hour and a half.

I share the victim impact statement so that you can see the totality of my case and feelings about it. In my opinion, the statement, combined with my appearances at every hearing related to my case, had impact on how the judge and DA handled the dispensation of the case. Since the statement was also included for probation, they had access to information they otherwise would never know.

It is difficult to describe the impact of domestic violence, as it is not always visible physically and the emotional damage is much deeper than any bruising ever could be. I am aware that I appear to be "all together". It is the only way for me to protect myself emotionally.

Since becoming a victim, I am suffering from PTSD and have been diagnosed as such by a licensed therapist who specializes in treatment of victims of abuse and domestic violence. My physical symptoms include shaking at the sight of Brian Massey or even the anticipation I might see him. My insides feel as if they are turning to jelly and it is a feeling of inner collapse. Sleeplessness and panic attacks that are so extreme; I am often too exhausted after work to do anything at all. I go to bed and sleep for a few hours, only to wake thinking someone is in my home or from nightmares. My nervous system is on high alert and every sound at night makes me afraid. Before this crime, I had none of these symptoms whatsoever.

I am someone who has always considered herself to be a strong and confident, professional woman. After one year of Brian Massey's emotional, intellectual and verbal abuse, I now depend on a therapist and my physician to regularly help me define correct decisions and treatment so that I can function at a diminished capacity day to day. I take anti-anxiety medication, something I am against in principle, due to being averse to pharmaceuticals, but something I cannot choose to do or not do because I cannot function properly due to extreme anxiety that often begins with no warning.

An attack of the kind that was perpetrated on me by Brian Massey has left me always looking over my shoulder. I cannot take walks without being afraid because I was threatened with violence. The night prior to the violence, Brian told me "I can do anything I want to you; nobody in this town is going to help you. The police are my friends." Seeing his rage and hearing the disgusting things he said to me are forever ingrained in my mind. It is going to take me a long time to repair the damage to my perception of myself that he worked so hard to destroy with his continual verbal insults, rewriting of history and frightening behaviors that shook me to my core.

The kind of effect this sort of experience has had on me is life altering. I am terrified that if I go on a hike alone, I will see Brian on a trail and that he will kill me.

I did see him one day when I was out hiking with a friend and it shook me to my core. No person should have to experience these kinds of fears, yet I will not be bullied out of this place I now call my home.

Brian beat his ex-wife so badly her face was badly bruised. (Alaska Court Records) Several women have come forward since my attack to tell me of Brian's rage when they dated him or had sexual relations with him. One was left so bruised, she never saw him again.

One burned toast in his kitchen in 2012 and angered him to the extent that she immediately left his home for the airport and never came back. She is now our city tax assessor. When she came to work in Sitka, she told me Brian came to her office specially to see her and inform her he was getting married to "a woman who keeps his temper in check." She was so intimidated by his visit; she tries to avoid seeing him on any level.

One need not actually experience the abuse to be traumatized. Just knowing that Brian has abused, and traumatized others adds to my fear and concern for my safety and well-being. I have no *guarantee he will not re-visit the violence toward me if he thinks he will get away with it.*

Brian has proven through past history that he cannot control his rage or his addictions. He uses alcohol in extreme amounts, is a former cocaine addict and also uses marijuana almost constantly. I doubt any kind of treatment will be effective for long as he has already completed rehab at least three times. Last summer when his mother died, the first thing he did was to confiscate her pain medications and he used them in dangerous combinations with alcohol, Ambien and Ativan.

I warned him he could die in his sleep if he was not careful, as he would begin choking in the middle of the night due to combining prescriptions that had not been written for him. He became very angry at me for saying this and verbally abused me for raising the issue. Although the doctor requested Brian return all unused medications, he refused to do so.

This prevented me from protecting myself towards his substance abuse, as talking about it became out of the question.

Last summer, weeks after my relocation to Sitka I discovered Brian was still communicating via email and Facebook with other women he had dated and had not informed them that he was engaged. This was taking place at his dying mother's bedside, while I was lifting her on and off the toilet. This past March, I found four pairs of women's panties in his dresser that were not mine. He refused to promise that it would not happen again and instead blamed me for jealousy. He has absolutely no compassion for having hurt me so deeply. I retain photos of these on my phone as a reminder that I should not trust or believe anything he says to me. This experience damaged my ability to trust my most intimate partner and my own judgement.

Brian is unable to take responsibility for his battering and addictions as evidenced by his past history of DV and his inability to face the consequences for what he has done to me, his ex-wife, and his single biggest victim, his own daughter. By her own account, she had to hold her mother, while she collapsed on her floor, bleeding from her face after her father beat her.

She has had to lie for him and as a trauma survivor, is now set up for a lifetime of abusive relationships that will stem from watching her father be an addict, a batterer, a liar, a manipulator, a cheat and an alcoholic. This has been extremely distressing to me as I felt his abuse being perpetuated on his daughter and re-experienced it all over again.

She has already started on her path to trouble with a DUI conviction last fall. My heart breaks for a beautiful and innocent female who is yet another victim of Brian's example of destruction of family and women. Brian sees himself as the victim in every case and has related many stories to me where he takes no ownership for his actions and in fact blames the very women he has victimized. He has almost every antisocial trait listed in the diagnosis of the personality disorder and I believe, will continue to hurt and abuse women for as long as he can get away with it.

Brian has a childhood history of trauma but is unwilling to do the work to change his behavior despite my pleading for us to go to counseling or do the work required to adjust his behaviors and actions. He steadfastly refused, telling me I am the one who needs to be fixed, not him.

I did attend a couple of sessions with a counselor prior to Brian's attack on me and she did warn me that my relationship was a classic abusive relationship and advised me to seek out a separate residence until I could work out the issues we were having. Still, I could not bring myself to abandon Brian, as I saw his alcoholism and drug abuse progressing.

I still love Brian deeply and was committed to our relationship as evidenced by my moving all the way to Sitka from New York to

*begin our life together. I did not abandon him. He abandoned me
the night he attacked me and broke his word and every promise
he made. Three days after his arrest he was emailing a former
lover in Anchorage, Alaska, showing me that I had no value to
him now that he had destroyed our life together.*

*I also retain a photo of his email to her from his iPad on my phone
as yet another reminder that he is not to be trusted.*

*Since most every element of trust and honesty was violated in
the context of my relationship with Brian, I am not able to trust
people any longer and this has also forced me to mistrust even
myself. After all, I thought I had chosen a man who would love,
honor and protect me. He had no intention of keeping his word
or his promises as evidenced by his behaviors and actions.*

*Finally, I would like to add that I am not without compassion and
understanding for Brian, as I too was a victim of early childhood
trauma and abuse. The difference between Brian and me is that
I have worked hard not to repeat the cycle, to take responsibility
for myself and not hurt or victimize others, as evidenced by my
lack of any form of interaction with the legal system and my large
circle of family and friends both in New York and in Sitka, who
love and support me. It is only through consequences that Brian
Massey will ever change, and maybe not even then.*

*I implore you to consider imposing the maximum consequence
on Brian for his crime of Criminal Mischief. I also request that I
receive restitution for the damage to my property in the amount
of $8,729, so that I may replace it and for the therapy I have had
to pay for in the amount of $2,000 that is not covered under my
health insurance plan.*

Thank you for giving me the opportunity to speak.

Dear reader, if you ever suffer this kind of misfortune with an abuser, I highly recommend including a statement, if not reading it at the sentencing. It might not only be cathartic; it also forces the perp to hear what they have done to you. It supplies information the judge may not otherwise have considered, as the DA is limited in what evidence the judge will actually permit. It may also aid probation in their efforts at managing the case and inform people otherwise not aware of the circumstances, such as family members the abuser has probably lied to, or at the very least, minimized his crime. He had emailed his priest, stating he was in shock at the consequences he was facing for damaging "a few items of his fiancée's clothing".

His sisters were present in the courtroom looking somber, slumped in their seats, mouths shaped like big, round O's, eyes glazed over seemingly amazed at the intensity of the proceeding. So was his stepfather, who up until that time, would not look me in the eye in passing at the grocery store or anywhere else. His stepmother, a woman I had been particularly fond of, asked me why I had not simply removed myself from the situation. I explained that had it been any of her daughters or even her granddaughter, she would not have tolerated the abuse for one minute. At least she acknowledged that at some point, people have to take responsibility for their actions. It was clear when after almost one and a half hours, the family knew Brian was the perp in the case despite stories he had told them.

When at last, Brian, wearing his courtroom "uniform" suit of a blue jacket and taupe slacks, spoke, he addressed the judge, not me, after his attorney offered that he wanted to apologize to me.

He rose from his seat with great effort, and with the demeanor of an elderly man looking pained, he said in raspy, barely audible voice, "Your Honor, I'm sorry for what I did. It was a crime." He sat back down immediately, never once looking my way.

In his book, *The Trauma Bond*, Patrick Carnes, Ph.D., explains that when a victim of abuse stands up and holds an abuser accountable, they must be prepared for the family to disown and even blame them for the crime.

All of this happened, as no family member ever bothered to call, text or email me after the attack to inquire about my well-being or needs. If they had, I could assure you my anger and desire to prosecute Brian would have been diffused. A shred of decency or compassion tossed my way would have had me begging the DA for mercy.

"People do not become who they are in a vacuum," my therapist said in an effort to help me understand the family's actions.

If I had to guess, including the loss of his job and attorney fees, the crime cost Brian close to $100,000. Although the consequences seemed minimal to me, I have to agree that he paid dearly for behaving like an ass.

Even more, the loss of the little respect he did have from the community was gone. For a man that counted appearances as so important, this had to be crushing. Still, he had his fat bank account and beautiful home to soothe his pain.

In relating earlier experiences to my relationship with Brian, you might see why I had delayed reactions and perhaps none, at times when I should have left the relationship. The attack on my clothing set off years of delayed reactions, allowing a more appropriate reaction this time due to therapy, a twelve-step program and knowledge acquired later in life. To be clear, Brian was certainly not my first relationship where abusive tendencies manifested, but because I had relocated all the way to Alaska and was without an established support system of friends and family, I tolerated more severe abusive behavior longer and felt less confident in leaving him. I was not aware of the SAFV shelter then and might have turned to them if I had known I could have. Still, I loved Brian and did not want to give up hope.

We each had our secrets, I'm sure. But he never asked about mine and he had no knowledge of my overflowing relationship baggage either.

Know this: It is important to understand our histories of love—in impressions, perceptions, reality and fantasy, what we want from love, and how we love others. All this starts with how we love ourselves.

I had learned through decades of experience, set in motion by my parents' treatment, unfortunately, to subject myself to others' preferences; that I did not matter and had been shamed enough times to see it as a part of life that was real and totally normal.

My childhood years faded away and my parents divorced when I was fourteen. By that time, Dad was in the throes of alcohol and cocaine abuse and had bigger fish to fry. I discovered his extramarital affair and told my mother.

Protecting me was not in the forefront of anyone's mind. I had been exposed to my best friend's father purposefully (I understood years later) leaving his bathrobe open to my seeing his privates. One day, I accidentally found my father's porn collection while in his workshop. *Hustler* magazine was much more graphic than *Playboy*, and he had quite a collection of child porn, too. These were my first exposures to sexual images and the behavior around it.

I was touched inappropriately by a great-uncle at age fourteen, when I had fully developed breasts. He approached me from behind, grabbing and rubbing my breasts, asking, "Where did you get these?" I threw his hands off, reacting in shock and horror at his groping and shouted for him to get away from me.

Soon, I informed my mother as I had been taught to do. Her response took my breath away. "That never happened," she said. I am sure she was shocked and caught off guard at my confession. "He never did that to me," she added.

I was too confused and hurt at her betrayal and refusal to protect me to think about what had happened, let alone wonder why she applied what he had done to me, to herself. Suddenly, in that split second, the fabric of my life was torn. I was alone. Years later, I would understand I felt it was a betrayal, a theme repeated during life. For many years to come, this moment of betrayal as I felt it, would be repeated as I unconsciously gave Mother, through others, the chance to undo it and take my side. Nobody ever would protect me. It took me until I turned fifty years old to understand that nobody was coming to save me. I would have to save myself.

When I promptly told my grandmother what her brother had done, she said, "Joe, if you ever touch her again, I will kill you." Most people didn't challenge Ida.

She couldn't always be there, however.

When I was 15 years old, after I was raped by a neighbor's brother, I simply went home and took a shower. He told me nobody would believe me, and I believed him. He was about seven years older than I was and his wild black hair and eyes scared me. I kept it a secret until I was 45 years old and remembered the attack after a therapist persuaded me to think about that age and what might have happened to me in that time period. It rose up out of nowhere, a totally forgotten event I had minimized and tucked away. When my rapist died years earlier, a victim of a motorcycle accident, I even attended his funeral with my mother, never thinking about what he had done to me. To this day, I cannot ride on a motorcycle.

Somehow, through all of this, I kept my fantasy of love and finding Prince Charming alive. My innocence and belief in love stayed intact despite evidence that proved otherwise. I refused to give it up, even more determined to find that magic man and the love that would give my life meaning beyond all other things.

I found myself at age 15, involved with a man ten years my senior and I wanted to be safe and protected, thinking someone older would do that.

Relationships with imbalances of power are doomed and this one dissolved by the time I turned 18 and looked for brighter horizons. However, I was technically raped and taken advantage of. I was a child, and looking back, he was sick to even think of initiating me into sex that age. A pathological liar and dishonest older man, he pulled the wool over my eyes many times and took advantage of a young, innocent woman looking for a safe haven.

Years of inappropriate, damaged and broken relationships followed. I was unable to see the early connection of the traumas and how they affected my choices. For example, at the age of 19, I married a man who was 46, and he wanted to me engage in sexual threesomes with him and a girlfriend of mine. I refused. The marriage collapsed and we divorced within six months, after he disclosed that he had also been a victim of childhood sexual abuse.

Several relationships with older men followed, but I was single until when, at age 35, I married a man much older than me who shortly after the wedding, confessed to becoming a victim of prolonged sexual abuse as a child. His distorted views, paranoia and sexual desires for bizarre acts brought that marriage to an end quickly. Police were involved and mental health was also an issue for him.

I also had a few pleasant experiences with men I had no passion for. They were kind, gentle and probably normal. They did not fit my perception and I felt bored without the dysfunction, chaos, arguing and substance abuse I had witnessed in my parents' own marriage and my relationships to date. I was a mercenary, dating and sorting, working so hard to make my fantasy come true, still believing.

Early experiences color our perceptions and create our unique worlds. My constant fantasizing of a Rhett Butler-type man had kept me hoping.

Years of emotion and passion were unleashed as I worked diligently to prosecute Brian and probably every man that I had known in my lifetime that had done me wrong. Still, he was gone. I felt frozen, still living in our home and having absolutely no idea where I was going. I set my intention to stay in Sitka at least until the case was resolved and I was better able to cope. Having been brought to my knees emotionally, I work hard daily to learn about addiction and abuse so that my pattern of destructive relationships is never again repeated.

In late September, a new interim director of behavioral health started at the hospital where I worked in Sitka. Frank was striking, with blue eyes like pools of water and he was of the dark and handsome variety. I ignored him but had the occasion to meet with him in his office to discuss recruitment. As the meeting wound down after close to two hours, he blindsided me by saying, "You are a very attractive woman and I'd like to spend some time with you."

I had mixed feelings and was still very much involved in the case against Brian, knowing it would not wrap up until year-end. Frank was patient, kind and supportive of me, holding me up when I was weak and unsure. While his translucent blue eyes and dark skin looked so familiar, I could not put him in context in Alaska.

"Where are you from?" I asked. "What is your ethnicity?"

"Italian. Calabrese. I'm from Pittsburgh," he replied. With similar ethnic backgrounds (I am almost half Calabrese) and East Coast origination, I had to know more.

On our first date, I felt compelled to tell him of the circumstances of my most recent breakup four months earlier. His background in psychology and therapy, as well as his skilled insights, and understanding, accelerated my healing. We hiked, enjoying nature in Sitka, and often fished with mutual friends.

Soon, we would say goodbye in Sitka as he departed to Minnesota. ...And I headed back to New York to rebuild my life.

In the meantime, I quit my job in October, unable to work at the hospital due to my PTSD, which caused me great irritability and also knowing it was a bad fit. I gave two weeks' notice, collected some vacation pay and moved on almost one year to the date of my hire.

The herring spawned. I still watched from my window as the big blue boat came and went weekly, knowing I was not yet done in Alaska.

CHAPTER 23

Dark Archives

"Resilience is, of course, necessary for a
warrior. But a lack of empathy isn't."
— *Phil Klay*

OTHER VICTIMS HAVE taught me about the depth and breadth of domestic violence. I share some of their thoughts in hopes that if you are a victim, you might hear something that makes you feel less alone, isolated, ashamed or different. While I did not endure physical injury, the damage was severe and lasting. I interviewed others who wanted to share their experiences so that you know you are not alone.

Most victims want anonymity. They are scared and Sitka is a small town. I respect their willingness to share and educate all of us so that we can learn valuable insights. The following stories and experiences have been shared with me out of a genuine concern for other women. My desire is to out these men and shame them. We do not deserve the shame nor should we hide; they should.

"Greta" shared that she had been involved with three abusive men in her history. One of them is the father of her youngest son. He has a mental illness but has also been charged with two rapes and recently been released from prison. Although he is in another state, he began to harass her once again, emailing her the lyrics from a Blue October song, "The End", depicting a murder-suicide after a man catches his woman cheating.

Greta obtained a three-year restraining order, but when mental illness is a component of DV, things can deteriorate and become frightening. Imagine receiving the lyrics of a song about murder and revenge and what one might do, the choices each of us might be faced with when threats such as this are clearly made.

Greta had no way to know what her ex would do next. She had a 4-year-old to care for and was busy with her day-to-day life. She had so many reasons to be concerned, yet the protections in place were flimsy at best.

Sarah also shared her experience in detail. She was fortunate to have gotten out alive. Her partner not only physically and sexually assaulted her—he also told her where he would bury her after he killed her:

> When I was in my early teens, I read a story about a woman who was a victim of domestic violence. Her husband beat, raped and maimed her. Eventually, she found the courage to leave the situation. I remember thinking to myself that the woman was an idiot. What kind of person would stay with someone who was so cruel to them?
>
> Fast forward ten plus years—it was a cold night in January when I found myself in a similar situation—realizing that exodus was my only option.
>
> I grew up in a rural ranching community in Eastern Oregon with my parents and four sisters. Our home life was stable and close knit. After graduating from high school, I moved across the state

to go to college. I was accepted into nursing school and while I was there met the boyfriend that would become my husband.

He was incredibly charming, with deep brown eyes and a sense of humor. I never met anyone that didn't like him. He came from a well-respected and established family that was supportive of our relationship. There were a lot of ups and downs, but he never did anything early on that gave me any idea he could be a monster. Not wasting any time, we got married in the fall after graduation. He was a civil engineer and we relocated to the city so that he could pursue his career. While the job went wonderfully, he was miserable living there. He sank into a depression, gained weight and started drinking. We lived there a little over a year and then decided to move to a different part of the state. It would be closer to his family and would get him out of his funk. We bought a big house with lots of space and dreamed about raising our family there.

If he was miserable in the city, it became worse when we moved.

Nothing was ever good enough. We started arguing more. The drinking escalated and he was drinking a fifth every few days. With the drinking came words and accusations that were hurtful and unexpected.

The first time he hit me we were standing in the kitchen arguing about something. I remember the stunned feeling as his fist hit my arm. I looked at him, took my purse and left. That night, I stayed with my friend, watching the red mark on my left arm turn to a bruised purple. The next day, I went home to flowers, apologies and a new Coach bag. We signed up for counseling.

Our first counselor taught therapy groups for domestic violence offenders and was incredibly helpful. We watched her draw the cycle of violence and talked about healthy relationships, how we could make ours better. It helped ... for a while things improved. And then they got worse again.

It was a slow decline. There were good days and bad. His fuse became shorter. When a pipe in the bathroom leaked water through the wall, he screamed and punched a hole through the sheetrock. Everything was my fault. I spat back but eventually learned it was just easier to stay out of the way. Things took a turn when he was injured and then had to rely on me for almost everything.

He played rugby on the weekends and ended up breaking his leg. He yelled at me in the hospital and screamed that if I wasn't "such a dumb fucking cunt, his goddamn leg wouldn't be broken". Confined to the recliner and limited in his ability to move, he would hiss insults from his chair and berate me for not doing things correctly. He was angry and annoyed with everything and everyone.

Several weeks later, I cooked dinner for my sister, her boyfriend and one of my husband's friends. Before dinner he and his friend were mixing drinks and polished off an entire bottle of vodka before we sat down to eat. He became ill and when I went into the bathroom to help him, he used the crutch to slam the door and started screaming at me. He pinned me up against the wall and beat my legs with his crutches, yelling and shouting in my face about what a worthless fucking cunt I was and how I made him sick. I stood there frozen and trapped; everything just stopped and buzzed. My sister and her boyfriend walked in about that time and that seemed to snap him back to reality. Her boyfriend came in and pulled him off of me.

There are a million little things that happened around that time. The words he would say to me, the way he would twist my arm or scream and spit in my face.

How he locked me out of the house on a snowy November night for a few hours. The punch to my stomach and the twist down the stairs. The time, he flushed my jewelry down the toilet. The way he said nobody else would want me because I was so hideous. Fingers twisting my hair because it was too goddamn short. How stupid I was. A broken bottle cutting into my arm. The bag of lime, the shovel and the towel in his truck that he said he would use to bury me in the desert. My friend, Yvonne, quietly asking if I was okay and how I lied and said yes because I knew what she would say. The time he threw the hammer at me and called me a bitch in front of our neighbor. Flowers.

The spot past the milepost when he nonchalantly said, "If you ever die, I am going to put you there." Whiskey breath, bloodshot eyes and words in my face. New Year's Eve when he drove home from work at 11:00 in the morning and was so intoxicated that it's a miracle he even made it. A million little excuses that I made. The point where I didn't really even care because I knew I was trapped. The apologies, the tears and the gifts. So many little things that eventually added up. It was like a glass that starts with a few expanding cracks that eventually explode and shatter.

I said things I shouldn't have. While I never resorted to violence, I had my own reserve of insults to fling back. I didn't tell people because I knew if I did, they would ask me why I put up with it, why I didn't leave and ask what I did to deserve it. There was the house, the mortgage, the money, our families—nobody else in my family was divorced. It was easy for me to push his buttons and sometimes I would. It was my fault. Or was it? What happened to the sweet man I married? I felt lost, lonely and stuck. I hated him. I loved him. Maybe it was me? I turned myself on auto pilot. I couldn't think, I could barely breathe, and I didn't see a way out of the situation; after all, I was the one who chose it. It was the life I had wanted. Right? I was so tired.

The last straw was the day after New Year's Eve. We joined a group of friends for drinks at the local brewery and came home. He was agitated when we got home because he thought I was too flirty with one of our friends. He started yelling, we started fighting and the next thing I knew I was slammed up against the wall. Then I was on the floor and there was a pillow over my face and pain.

Screaming.

Arms.

Slamming.

Floor.

Blood.

Face down.

In my head I left. I wasn't there.

Later, I found myself huddled in a dark corner of the room, trembling and bruised when I thought it. What if I had a baby? It was a moment of complete clarity. I realized there was no way it was going to work. My only option was leaving. We were going to have a family....and there was no way I could do that with that man. If I stayed, I was going to die.

I didn't cry. I sat there stunned. I called my friend at work and told her what happened. I knew if I told someone, especially about that time, I would have to do something about my situation. She offered to call the police, but I was afraid of what he would do after they left.

The next day I told him I wanted a divorce. He cried, begged and pleaded. Finally, he left and went to stay with his parents. The next few weeks were a blur. I got divorce papers quickly in order. He was on best behavior, quit drinking and refused to sign anything. His parents found us a Christian counselor that I agreed to go to. The first thing I told her was that we were getting divorced and I rolled up my sleeves so she could see my bruised arms. She laughed nervously and then straightened her pen and told me that Jesus really didn't want us to get divorced but obviously we needed to work on some things. I walked out.

He continued to refuse to sign the papers, so I took things into my own hands. One Thursday night, I went out to the bar and went home with someone else. The next day he moved out. He told his family I had an affair. I knew that if it was my fault and he had an excuse he would leave. I was at the point where I didn't care and would do whatever it took to get out of the situation.

He signed the papers, and it was over...until a few weeks later when he contacted me. He was smashed out of his mind and told me if the ass-beating he gave me was bad before, he was coming over and it would be worse. That led to a restraining order, and then it really was over.

I had to report the restraining order to my work. It was stressful. It was embarrassing. I found myself responsible for the house and the mortgage payment which was over half of my income. He took all the furniture, most of the money and any security that was there. There were numerous times that I would sit on the tiled floor in the kitchen sobbing, drinking glasses of tequila and smoking cigarettes.

I threw wild, crazy parties and wandered around bleary eyed and completely lost. It was like I had lived my life to that point as a zombie and I had woken up to a nuclear world that I didn't understand and didn't know what to do with. I cried, I laughed, I danced, I fucked, I lit things on fire and tried to find myself.

When everything you think your life is supposed to be suddenly cracks open and you're left with the ashes of it all, it is a strange thing. It was liberating, sad, terrifying and it took every ounce of who I was to work through that situation.

The short story is that eventually things got better. I went through *hours of therapy. I had co-workers who helped me immensely; I ran and burned through so many things. I worked. I traveled. I met someone. I moved. I changed.*

I think about what happened every day. There are random moments where I feel the wall against my head, sharp words against my face and a twist in my arm.

I read about things that happen in the world and I feel how minute my situation is. Some days, I feel so angry. Some days, I forget. There are times when even though I know none of it was my fault, it still feels like it was. It is strange and challenging to talk about it, but I want so desperately to.

CHAPTER 24

The Fantasy is at Rest

*"Very often a change of self is needed
more than a change of scene."*

—*A.C. Benson*

EACH WEEK, AS the ferry slipped in and out of town, I wondered how long I would wait to leave Sitka. I looked longingly at that boat, knowing my days there were numbered, believing with all my heart that I would know the right time to say goodbye to this beautiful island in the North Pacific Ocean, a land of extremes. A land that stole my heart with its unfailing ability to surprise and delight my senses daily with new natural wonders and mystical, ethereal beauty.

Emotions were like the highest and longest roller coaster, varying from love to hate, back to love again. I know there was no possibility of a future with a man like Brian, but still, I had staked everything I had on the love I believed we had and the future he so glowingly described. Such a thing is the hardest of all things to give up on.

I did not always behave properly. After being victimized, no one does. My only excuse is to say that functioning with PTSD is a compromised state of being, where reason and emotion often compete for attention. I was also livid. I did what I felt I had to in the moment and am still not sure I would do anything differently today. I mailed the perpetrator a few angry letters and sent emails expressing both love and hate.

I dreamt of revenge, of reuniting, of his approaching me and apologizing...it went on and on and on until one day, while at a local gathering, a single woman who recognized me from my days with Brian approached me with info that he had been blowing up the dating app, Tinder, just three days prior to the party. All of a sudden, I realized I had done nothing to cause the events that took place between us. He was repeating his pattern of cheating on yet another unsuspecting woman. I felt relief and finally release from the prison I had held myself hostage in for close to this entire past year. Still, I had no comprehension of what would come next or how to put my life back together.

One day, in quiet meditation, I heard a voice. This experience had only happened to me few times in life, but when it does, I listen. It said, "It is not outside of you." Wow. Profound, especially for a woman that had always looked outside of herself for fulfillment and happiness. My inner voice. My knowing. I didn't need a name for it.

From that moment, I was at peace in myself and have continued to be at peace from a lifelong place of unrest and searching for someone to give me, maybe tell me, that I was enough, was loved, wanted; something I no longer needed to fill what I referred to as the "big black hole of need".

The fantasy is at rest.

After so many attempts, I do not believe I failed; rather, I have come to know that not everyone is meant to meet, marry and settle down as society so trains us to believe. I realized that some of us have other purposes that may not include those experiences. If my life were an example of this, I accepted it wholeheartedly. It was a kind of freedom.

I worked on forgiveness. I didn't want to live in the war zone of hatred and jealousy any longer. My former partner, Brian, sported around town with a new woman. I saw her Facebook posts as they traveled to places that I thought I would go with him, experiences I believed we should have had before the trouble started.

My heart leaped out to her because after he showed his best side first, the insults and slights would begin anew, and work their way up the cycle until he hurt her, too. Soon, after he dumped her for another, younger woman, I would know again. The story was the same.

I prayed to the god of my understanding for help. Several times, while on walks alone in the forest I asked for this unseen, but not unfelt, help. The power of the sprit comforted me. This alone made the trip to Alaska worth its weight in gold. I asked for help at forgiveness, being a better person and for all my choices. I had gone it alone, inside myself, for as long as I could remember. I knew with no doubt I was not alone, and the wild unpredictability of Alaska taught me this.

CHAPTER 25

Answers in the Forest

"There is no medicine like hope, no incentive so great, and no tonic so powerful as expectation of something better tomorrow."
—*Orison Swett Marden*

FILLED WITH YELLOW cedar, hemlock and Sitka spruce, the forest floor is blanketed in mossy green cover and a wet mist. Waterfalls and huge trees line the coast of Alaska's gulf and inside passage.

Residents value the outdoor life, and the trails are impeccably maintained, circling lakes and mountains in the foreground, spongy musk egg earth under foot.

The sound of water moving and dripping everywhere out of the ground and off of the tree branches lends a mystical quality to the forest, droplets of diamonds hanging from the needles and sunlight gleaming through the trees in misty beams feels deeply spiritual to me. I noticed more than once that being in nature is in direct conflict with negative emotion. It is the grand healer. No matter my mood, once out there, negativity vanishes.

The rain is cleansing, refreshing, and essential for the survival of all. Perhaps it was that amount of water that took me out of myself, just long enough to be clean again and start over.

Maybe the reason I went to the small fishing village of Sitka, Alaska where it rains in such extreme amounts that the water just runs out of cliffs, streams and rocks everywhere in the Tongass Forest, as if the earth would burst from holding so much was a message: I don't have to bleed out everything I have to be of value.

Until now, that seemed unclear. While getting rid of even more of my possessions, as I prepared to depart Sitka, it became as clear as the North Pacific, which if you have not been there, is deep, frigid and crystalline.

Rain is cleansing, refreshing, and essential for the survival of all. Perhaps it was that amount of water that took me out of myself just long enough to be clean again and start over.

In early July, I boarded the ferry in Sitka for the two-day trip to Prince Rupert, British Columbia. On the ferry with me, was a friend from Sitka who was moving to Ketchikan. We watched the magnificent beauty of Alaska as we floated by for miles and miles stopping to view the Fourth of July fireworks in Wrangell, Alaska, another lovely town. I felt some regret as I wondered if I might ever again see the awesome beauty of this place that I had been so privileged to be a part of, a place where I experienced an awakening. A place that so changed me, I had no idea how life would look when I got "home". Brilliant skies, calm water and green passed me by for hours as we cruised. Leaving Sitka was akin to leaving a much-loved family member.

British Columbia is a wild and awesome place of beauty. I drove 500 miles each day at the start of my journey through places with very little population. Forests, desert and mountains were all in my scope along the way. Flowers blooming and endless fields that seemed to stretch on forever, one hundred and eight degrees around me. Even Alaska was not this expansive. It was simply too much for my senses to comprehend. Part of me wanted to get lost in this land and stay hidden. I felt this several times on my journey. Some places feel more like home than others, and there were a few I could have lived in for the rest of my days.

Finally, when I thought I could not see another beautiful river, bright green from glacial runoff, I reached the US border at Washington State and handed my passport to the border agent. "Welcome to the United States," he said.

That night, I slept in a tiny motel with paper-thin walls and had a Mexican dinner overlooking the ocean and preparing myself for the drive down the coast and into Oregon, hoping to meet friends from Sitka to spend a few days with and rest with for the remaining trip across the United States, ending in the Hudson Valley area of New York, the place I had started this journey from two and a half years earlier.

Driving is cathartic. Every passing mile I put between myself and Brian healed me. Recovery came in fits and starts, and mine was no different. Thoughts of whether I had done the right thing ran though my head, but with each passing mile, I felt more and more at home with my choices.

Three days on the misty Oregon coast with two friends, who I had met in Alaska, was wonderfully comforting.

Oregon is a beautiful state to drive through and the wine country of the Willamette Valley, combined with the huge rock outcroppings along the coast, made for dramatic views unlike any other. The rain and mist gathering offshore made it even more alluring. I could have stopped right there.

My ocean-view inn and Nye Beach were cozy and warm. Town was so relaxed and many of the residents sported long white ponytails and wore leather sandals. Lovely restaurants with healthy fresh food lined the streets of Newport. Food is organic, fresh and delicious in Oregon, as no pesticides are used in farming; a fact I would later learn at the California border when I would be forced to hand over a five-pound bag of luscious cherries to the agriculture patrol!

The trip took eighteen days. I drove across the middle of the country on I-80 and took my time. Time to think and ponder, time to heal and let go; time to contemplate my future and who might be in it.

My only child, Trevor, was supportive and loving despite his anger at my having left New York in the first place. Early on, after my first visit to Sitka, my son made a prescient statement after seeing just one photograph of Brian. "He has rage, Mom, and very high blood pressure."

My son set me free from my guilt at not heeding his advice completely by informing me that I needed to go make a life. Even though I was not sure where that was at the moment, he said I knew and that I only had to let my heart tell me where. Where I did it, he was not invested in. He had a life as an adult and knew that once my life was stable again, we would be even closer than we had ever been. His gift released my guilt and anguish over not having been there these last few years.

Overflowing with relief and rejuvenation to be in New York, I re-connected with dear friends, became gainfully employed and did my best to make good choices and to repair the fabric of my life and myself.

Best of all, I fell in love. Is he husband material? I'll never use that goddamned phrase again!

I had another chance to make the life I now believed I was entitled to have; one where I do matter and one where I am loved. One where I have enough. I no longer have the need for hundreds of thousands of dollars, but for a life that includes some measure of financial stability for me; a life that I create and maintain, caring for myself as I have always cared for others. I have never been perfect and have made many, many mistakes, but I have come to know that I have always done my best. And for now, that is enough.

Who does this make me now? Life has much to behold and always surprises me! I am stronger and feel clear and certain about me, the person I never knew.

Perhaps I am better prepared to see myself and admit to myself who I truly am. This takes courage. It is not easy to break out of a conventional mold of life that some of us have reduced ourselves to abide by.

I returned to real estate and am very busy. With the coronavirus raging as of this writing, about 15,000 Manhattanites left the city and flooded into Hudson Valley. I got engaged to a wonderful French-Canadian man that shares the same birthday as me. He does not touch alcohol because of his father's abuse of it. Self-made and a very successful individual. I didn't need a four-and-a-half carat diamond ring, but he wanted me to have it the minute he proposed. We met a month after I returned to New York. We sat and drank coffee for eight hours on our first date. Two years later, we moved in together. A psychic told us we would be together for a very long time.

I miss Alaska every single day. But my heart is bursting in New York again.

ABOUT THE AUTHOR

Adriana Jaymes grew up in the Hudson Valley area just north of New York City. She graduated from Marist College with a BS in Liberal Studies. Adriana has worked in real estate and banking for 35 years. Adriana has one son and lives with her partner while they renovate a mountaintop stone house as a mutual passion. *Running from Bears* is her debut book.